LEADING A CONGREGATION TO RELEVANCE

C. DEAN WATERMAN

WESTBOW
PRESS®
A DIVISION OF THOMAS NELSON
& ZONDERVAN

Copyright © 2022 C. Dean Waterman.

All rights reserved. No part of this book may be used or reproduced by any means, graphic, electronic, or mechanical, including photocopying, recording, taping or by any information storage retrieval system without the written permission of the author except in the case of brief quotations embodied in critical articles and reviews.

This book is a work of non-fiction. Unless otherwise noted, the author and the publisher make no explicit guarantees as to the accuracy of the information contained in this book and in some cases, names of people and places have been altered to protect their privacy.

WestBow Press books may be ordered through booksellers or by contacting:

WestBow Press
A Division of Thomas Nelson & Zondervan
1663 Liberty Drive
Bloomington, IN 47403
www.westbowpress.com
844-714-3454

Because of the dynamic nature of the Internet, any web addresses or links contained in this book may have changed since publication and may no longer be valid. The views expressed in this work are solely those of the author and do not necessarily reflect the views of the publisher, and the publisher hereby disclaims any responsibility for them.

Any people depicted in stock imagery provided by Getty Images are models, and such images are being used for illustrative purposes only.
Certain stock imagery © Getty Images.

Unless otherwise indicated, all Scripture quotations taken from the (NASB®) New American Standard Bible®, Copyright © 1960, 1971, 1977, 1995, 2020 by The Lockman Foundation. Used by permission. All rights reserved. www.lockman.org

Scripture quotations marked MSG are taken from The Message, copyright © 1993, 2002, 2018 by Eugene H. Peterson. Used by permission of NavPress. All rights reserved. Represented by Tyndale House Publishers.

Scripture quotations marked (ESV) are from the ESV® Bible (The Holy Bible, English Standard Version®), copyright © 2001 by Crossway, a publishing ministry of Good News Publishers. Used by permission. All rights reserved. The ESV text may not be quoted in any publication made available to the public by a Creative Commons license. The ESV may not be translated into any other language.

ISBN: 978-1-6642-7962-9 (sc)
ISBN: 978-1-6642-7963-6 (hc)
ISBN: 978-1-6642-7961-2 (e)

Library of Congress Control Number: 2022918094

Print information available on the last page.

WestBow Press rev. date: 10/17/2022

DEDICATION

To three mentors, and their wives, who have impacted my life and ministry with 150+ years of collective wisdom.

Henry and Carol Wright
Robert and Karen Fancher
John and Karen Cress

Contents

Acknowledgments ix
Before You Begin xi
Introduction xv

Chapter 1	Spiritual Leadership 1
Chapter 2	Do-Re-Mi 7
Chapter 3	The Model 12
Chapter 4	The Right Start 15
Chapter 5	Strategic Vision 22
Chapter 6	Congregational Management 30
Chapter 7	Intentional Discipleship 35
Chapter 8	Developing Leaders and Teams 42
Chapter 9	The Next Generation 51
Chapter 10	Communicating for Results 62
Chapter 11	Engaging the Body 69
Chapter 12	The Third Place 76
Chapter 13	The Prayer-Centric Congregation 86
Chapter 14	Nuts and Bolts of Relevancy 94
Chapter 15	Embracing Guests 107
Chapter 16	God-Centered Worship 115
Chapter 17	Measure what Matters 123
Chapter 18	Missional Influence 130
Chapter 19	The Teaching Ministry 140
Chapter 20	Decisions & Discipleship 146
Chapter 21	Exponential 155
Chapter 22	The Model Congregation 161
Chapter 23	Before You Go 164

A quick note … 169

Acknowledgments

To Jody, who has been a valued life and ministry partner for 25 years. You have endured much; from my personal failures and wounds from various sheep within the congregations we served together. I could not have done the work I have without you.

To my children, Joseph and Andrea, who didn't get as much of me as they deserved while in their formative years. I realized almost too late that ministry starts in the family, the congregation follows. I love both of you, and my ministry will be complete with both of you in heaven with your mother and me.

To my previous congregations. I feel pity for the ones who got me in the beginning of ministry, and I am sorry for being young, foolish, and too proud to learn from wise ones until later in ministry. For your patience, and kindness, thank you. For all my previous members, some who may still be upset with me just a little, I love you now as I did while pastoring with you.

To my sister, Rita, for cheerleading and editing this book. For maintaining my "voice" and passion, while making this book better than I even hoped. For always being a force for good and kindness the past five decades of life.

To my parents, Russell (deceased) and Joan Waterman, who listened to God's voice and took the boy home to foster, when they really wanted a girl. Then if that wasn't enough, you brought me into the family by adoption. It was a divine appointment, and while I had my rough patches, you survived!

To all colleagues and friends from the previous decades. Each of you know who you are, and I value all of you for your kindness, friendship, frankness, and willingness to humor me. For ministry colleagues, regardless of the denomination you serve, I cheer you on as all of us continue to serve God and love the people with a heart like Jesus. Soon the rewards will be evident.

Before You Begin

The story has been often told of a young elementary school girl sitting in art class one day. The teacher had given a specific assignment to draw whatever each young student wanted to share with others and their parents. As the teacher went from student to student observing their individual artwork, she looked over the shoulder of the young girl, and asked her, "What is this you are drawing?" The girl replied, "God." "That is quite impossible!" the teacher exclaimed, "For not one person knows what God looks like!" Head still down, drawing carefully, the girl simply replied, "They will when I am finished."

And therein lies the call for each of us as Christians, leaders, and our congregations today.

Painting a Portrait

One of my favorite authors, A.W. Tozer, writes the most profound sentence I have ever read. "What comes into our mind when we think about God is the most important thing about us."[1] To his statement I would add this; what we lead others to think about God may be equally important, if not more. As Christians, we have opportunities each day to shape other people's views of God. Within the context of this book, the same is true. Every congregation on this planet is painting a portrait of God to those who are watching.

Knowing that is the case leads to a most important question: what image of God is your congregation painting? It isn't just the sermons and worship service, but the interactions new guests have with members, and

---

[1] A.W. Tozer, *The Knowledge of the Holy* (New York: Harper One – Harper Collins, 1992), 1

members interacting with each other. It is how children come to see their value within the congregation, and adults just the same. It is seen in how "sinners" and backsliders are accepted or rejected and various opinions and viewpoints on faith are encouraged or discouraged. Within each respective community, congregations are ever revealing God as either One of infinite love, concerned with humans' everyday life, or who is aloof and non-existent amid the challenges present within culture today. Realize this: every action, or inaction, is a witness to what we believe God to be. So, then, what are people truly seeing through your congregation and mine as we reveal God to them?

This is Personal

I wrote this book because I love the congregations that dot the landscape of America, Canada, and around the world. I believe each one has a solemn responsibility to reflect God accurately to the world, and more specifically to their community. There may be numerous denominations created by barriers that have been self-imposed, but ultimately as the *ekkēlesia* (more on that later) we are called to the same purpose—reflect God to those who have never met Him or have a negative view of Him from a previous experience. Yet in many congregations, this has not been the case, but an afterthought. Many truths have been preached, without Jesus as the center of truth being preached. I was guilty of that for so long. Then I learned an important lesson personally. God is love. Everything else in the Bible just proves it. When I learned this fundamental truth for myself it changed my life, ministry, and outlook. It also changed the congregations I pastored after that point, proving to me congregations often reflect their leader(s).

That is why this book is personal. I love the church, and the congregations that make up the body of Christ. I want to see each one makes an impact on the lives of their members, each new guest, and their community. Why? Because each congregation is painting a portrait of God, and that includes yours too. For many congregations, the portrait they are painting is causing people to run away from God, not to Him. There is enough distortion in the world about who God is, and His attributes, without the church joining in. The challenge is recognizing where a congregation may be failing in this regard and changing it.

When my understanding of God personally changed from a "checklist"

God, who demanded things from me through obedience and compliance (legalistic) to be loved and ultimately saved, to one of unmeasurable love (grace), wow! No longer did my behaviors reflect earning God's love but reflected the gift of grace I was experiencing personally. My sermons took on new life. My congregation soon came to reflect on what I lived, believed, and preached about God. Before long the congregation began to grow. The portrait of God they were painting for others began to change, and it was attractive. Love was the brush that painted this new portrait of God. The congregation began to reflect what they believed about God individually as a result.

Now You Know

That is why I have written this book, so your congregation can do the same. I don't care what denomination you are. Where your congregation is located. What skin color you have or your members. I want the same for you as I have been able to experience. For you personally, and for the congregation you lead or are a member of. Personally, that you will come to know God as He desires to be known. That when you think of God, you will weep at the goodness of His love for you, those you serve, and the community outside the walls you are called to reach. For your congregation, that they will soon come to know God as you do, and as He desires to reveal Himself to them. When this happens, we won't need laws and regulations to change the outcomes in the communities each congregation exists in. They will have the church, the Body of Christ. Relevant congregations make a significant impact where they exist, and it is time all our congregations do just that.

I love God, I love the church, and it is my singular passion to assist congregations in being relevant. Furthermore, reflecting the love of God accurately, one that gives a beautiful portrait of love and truth to those in our world who are seeking both.

Introduction

Can a congregation be relevant? If so, what would be the measurements to define its relevancy?

> Increased attendance?
> Ministries and activities?
> Level of giving?
> Modern music?
> Facility location?
> Leadership style?

Ask different pastors and church leaders, and you will likely receive many varied answers about what defines a congregation's relevancy. Many might even dismiss the concept of relevancy and identify success simply as a healthy church growing by specified numbers. That's an old scorecard. The new one is relevance. I submit to you a definition that can apply to every congregation, one that can truly define a congregation on a mission for God, living out the meaning of the Great Commission:

A relevant congregation makes a significant spiritual impact on individual lives and the community it exists in, without condition. It does so by exhibiting the timeless message of the gospel, while ministering within the context of the culture and community it exists in.

Relevant congregations have a culture, or a DNA if you prefer, of genuine love, acceptance, and grace. It is a safe place, inclusive within their community for anyone who enters the doors. They join people on their journey of intentional discipleship from atheist to saint. They are welcoming of diverse perspectives, inviting conversations on personal faith and God. Irrelevant congregations do the opposite; "In a place where no one's allowed to ask questions, share doubts, engage in dialogue, or be completely honest, relevance simply can't exist."[2]

Relevant congregations welcome everyone; those with diverse opinions, faith journeys, lifestyles, and backgrounds. They are a "...map, directions, where people should look to find Me," in the words of Jesus as portrayed in the Dallas Jenkins produced streaming series, *The Chosen*.[3] This applies to those in the community who are discouraged and searching, looking for hope and meaning. They are looking for a relevant congregation who, "If someone wants to find me, those are the groups they should look for." These congregations model the principles of the Kingdom as Jesus taught in Matthew 5-7. They *exhibit* the gospel in action first, by word second.

Of course, this is my definition, but I stand by it. It comes from twenty-plus years in pastoral ministry and congregational leadership, leading thirteen congregations over that period. I've seen congregations on life support and congregations who are rays of relevance, impacting lives and their community. Some of the dying congregations I served had excellent financial reports. Others were doing well in attendance. Another was recognized in the community by its prominent location on the main street of town. A particular one was "hip" and perceived to be culturally relevant by music, casual dress, and an easily located coffee bar. In the case of each congregation, even when they met their specific numbers that would prove their success, it was easy to see they had lost relevance. They just didn't know it.

Why were they not relevant? Most weren't engaged in intentional discipleship and investing in the spiritual purpose and growth of the individuals who walked through their doors. They didn't speak to life as it is today, and the issues people deal with daily. Additionally, they were not outward focused on their community, living with missional influence. Most often this lack of outward focus was due to not understanding the culture and circumstances of their community. It became easier to remain insulated away from others than to reach out to them. While time and circumstances

---

[2] Thom and Joani Schultz, *Why Nobody Wants to Go to Church Anymore* (Loveland: Group, 2013), 26

[3] Season 2, Episode 8, 33:17-36:33

changed, the congregations rarely did. Therefore, when people came to visit these congregates, they experienced a message out of step with their life, and the challenges they were facing. These congregations I was involved with, and many other congregations I have observed, also seemed oblivious to the immense challenges within the culture, and preferred to ignore them, rather than address them with a biblical worldview.

These congregations weren't purposefully joining people on their spiritual journey and personal walk with God. These churches weren't missional, nor engaged in reaching the community with an actionable message of God's redeeming grace. The leaders and members did not obey Christ's command to be salt and light to a world needing both. They didn't exhibit the essential traits of biblical discipleship: unconditional love for others and all that entails, as Jesus taught (John 13:35).

In short, these congregations were not relevant. Not to individuals or the community the congregation was in. They existed. People attended. They made minimal spiritual impact.

Post-Pandemic View

This book comes from a post-pandemic viewpoint. At the time of this writing, in 2022, Barna Research Group stated 38 percent of pastors are considering leaving the ministry.[4] They are frustrated, dealt with many issues during the pandemic, and have seen their churches decline. Many members who quit attending church during the pandemic are not coming back. Multiple reasons exist for this, but I suggest the primary reason is that their church ultimately wasn't relevant in those people's lives. For whatever else COVID-19 brought about (and that list is long) telling the emperor he had no clothes may be the most significant. It may give us insight and some hope.

Ask people who are not back in attendance why they are not returning. One consistent answer is they found a service online, or another elsewhere, feeding them more than the church they attended pre-pandemic. Ouch! Imagine being that pastor (I have been) and hearing from members that they're never coming back because they found another church that feeds them better, another congregation that is relevant to them. The cliché, "Fed sheep don't

---

[4] https://www.barna.com/research/pastors-well-being/

wander." is true. Spiritually fed sheep won't wander when their congregation is relevant and intentional about being active in the lives of its members and living the Great Commission. As authors Thom and Joani Schultz quickly identify in these people who have left, never to return, they would tell us, if we will listen, "Your God is irrelevant in my life."[5] These individuals who left want, in essence, to "find the Divine in the world around us."[6] In short, they want relevance.

There is another reason why many congregations are viewed as irrelevant. Younger generations view the inclusion of all people as part of their daily lives. LGBTQ+, race and ethnicity, immigrant status, as well as social and economic status are of no matter if everyone is to be loved, respected, and allowed to be individualistic. Younger generations walk into congregations, see conditional acceptance, thus rejection, turn around, and walk right back out. Some to never enter a church building again. Political posturing, judgmental attitudes, and condemnation of lifestyle, dress, and other choices are more frequently on display from members than the unconditional love of Christ. Yes, we know what the Bible says. Still, in championing biblical truths, there is a tendency to judge and reject people while forgetting these important words of Jesus. "A new commandment I give to you, that you love one another, even as I have loved you, that you also love one another. By this, all men will know that you are My disciples if you have love for one another." John 13:34,35.

Many individuals abandoning congregations today because of its judgment and rejection of people have observed more acceptance in the world than in the church. They will leave and continue to find their safe "third place," wherever that leads them; be it in-person, online, or in the metaverse.[7] Wherever it takes them it will be expected to provide acceptance and recognition of a person's right to be who they are, unconditionally. It may not be a healthy space, but it accepts them for who they are; thus, they remain. They will go to where it feels relevant to their lives and connect with others who are seeking the same.

---

5   Thom and Joani Schultz, *Why Nobody Wants to Go to Church Anymore* (Loveland: Group, 2013), 26

6   Schultz and Schultz, 26

7   Oxford: "A virtual-reality space in which users can interact with a computer-generated environment and other users."

The Biblical Worldview Crisis

One last reason I will give for a congregation's lack of relevance is a misconstrued worldview that is not biblically based. Often this comes from the pulpit and the pastor leading the congregation, which eventually filters down to the leaders, and ultimately to the congregation. Increasingly congregations are being led by pastors who do not see the Bible as relevant to society and the cultural issues being dealt with today. This makes it increasingly difficult for members and attendees to find the Bible as relevant when the pastor preaching to them each week doesn't.

In a 2022 survey conducted by American Worldview Inventory[8], 1,000 pastors across the United States were asked about their beliefs and behaviors as they related to the Bible. In essence, their biblical worldview. The basis of a biblical worldview, as defined by the question, is the "adoption of the basic scriptural principles and teachings that form the filter through which we experience, interpret, and respond to the world." Some say life today is different than when the Bible was written, therefore the principles cannot apply. The survey responses prove this viewpoint.

Of those pastors who responded, only 37% have a biblical worldview. Reverse the statistic, and it indicates 63%, almost 2/3 of the pastors surveyed, and representative of the whole in the United States, do not hold a biblical worldview. These are the ones preaching every week, and their views are being preached and taught to millions of Christians as a result. The consequences to this restrained biblical worldview have become quite evident in the lives of many professed Christians. These individuals have taken a secular worldview in multiple areas of their lives, with some areas being politics, conflict-resolution, and education, to name a few. Rather than finding solutions to life through the lens of the Bible, they choose to use the world's remedies, most often to less than satisfactory results. This secular worldview has bled into many congregations, further blurring the line between the church and the world.

Read the survey results further and only 12% of youth pastors have a biblical worldview. This is quite alarming, as these are the ones entrusted to guide the next generation of Christians. Individuals pastoring in larger

---

[8] The Christian Post: Rethinking Your Relationships with the Church, Accessed July 10, 2022 https://www.christianpost.com/voices/rethinking-your-relationship-with-the-church.html

congregations of 250 in attendance or higher are less likely to have a biblical worldview than those pastoring in smaller congregations under 250. No matter what perspective by which these results are viewed, many congregations today are being led by pastors who no longer believe the Bible is relevant to life as we know it. If the Bible isn't relevant, this leads to potential doubt and questions regarding the relevance of God.

The Consistency of Change

While much is changing in the landscape of the church post-pandemic, and in the culture and community it exists in, I contend that some things will never change. There will always be questions about methodology and practices in reaching those outside of the building and for keeping those within the congregation from leaving. Still, one thing remains true: a relevant congregation will grow disciples, expand in influence, and impact their communities by being a "map" to God. In this age of technology, where everyone is blasted with media and ideas 24/7, the truth of any subject is getting more difficult to find, every heart is still seeking something that matters. Something that defines their purpose and ultimate reason for existence.

Augustine of Hippo, in 398 AD, wrote in *Confessions*, "You have made us for yourself, O Lord, and our hearts are restless until they rest in you." This was before a million things competed for a human's attention! In *Pensées*, published in 1670 by Blaisé Pascal, he gives further insight into the human state: "What else does this craving, and this helplessness, proclaim but that there was once in man a true happiness of which all that now remains is the empty print and trace. This he tries in vain to fill with everything around him, seeking in things that are not there, the help he cannot find in those that are, though none can help, since this infinite abyss can be filled only with an infinite and immutable object; in other words, by God Himself."

Currently, with much that competes for personal attention, whether in current reality or virtual reality, there are numerous questions about purpose and identity; questions about the ongoing violence and hate crimes, discrimination, and dismissal of others not like them. Real questions about God and His presence in a world gone to pieces. With all that people are facing, where are the relevant congregations available to help them discover God through the confusion of life today?

There is a clearly defined purpose and urgent need for relevant congregations. Congregations that champion the Bible as God's revelation of love, exhibit the gospel, lift up Jesus always, exude unconditional grace and acceptance, and purposefully join people on their journey of belief, or in some cases, lack of it. These congregation love all unconditionally, allowing the Holy Spirit to exercise the convictions on an individual's life. These relevant congregations walk with people as they search for meaning and purpose.

Missional congregations outward-focused, purposefully flowing into their community, walking along side people searching for meaning and purpose, and inviting them to a place at the table where they can find unconditional acceptance while they ask hard questions. Those congregations graciously welcome individuals who desire to openly explore their faith, converse candidly, and experience God personally.

Becoming Relevant

How can a congregation become relevant? What new methods and laboratory results can get a congregation there? What are the latest trends to adopt, the fad and worship format championed by the now-proclaimed church experts? Around the United States, I suspect hundreds of thousands of hours have been spent debating within church boards and leadership meetings as to what methods to adopt so their congregation can at least survive, and with some additional hope, thrive. John MacArthur may have identified the problem: "We are disastrously pragmatic. All we want to know about is what works. We want formulas and gimmicks, and somehow in the process we leave out that to which God has called us."[9] We have tendencies to keep up with those perceived to be ahead of us, chase after each new method and identify advanced creative thinking on the horizon to catch up to.

Methods alone do not make a congregation relevant. What the pastor wears when preaching, be it an untucked shirt and blue jeans, or a suit, doesn't make a congregation relevant. "Relevance isn't the worship pastor showing his tattoo on stage. Relevance isn't serving the fair-trade coffee in your lobby. Relevance isn't showing the latest popular movie clip during a sermon. True

---

[9] John MacArthur, *Worship: The Ultimate Priority* (Chicago: Moody, 1983, 2012), 51

spiritual relevance is being God in the matters at hand."[10] For this reason, we must drill down to what never changes in the search for relevance and impacting individual lives in the process.

It isn't what is new but rather what all along has been that matters most. Methods may change based on community, culture or denominational direction; fundamentals never will. Twenty years of experience and experiments have taught me a few things, with much of it learned by failure. I have listened to successful pastors, observed healthy, growing congregations, and researched best practices for measured success and missional relevancy. It always comes down to the fundamentals which you will read in the following pages.

In 2015 the denomination I served granted me a two-month sabbatical. One stipulation existed for this sabbatical—that of spiritual insight and growth. At the beginning of my two months, which our family spent traveling across the American West in a Fifth-wheel, camping at various national parks, I asked God to give me something that would make a difference in my pastoral ministry. I sketched the basics of my research and personal experience into what you will find here but then refined it over seven years to affirm what I originally put together. Since that sabbatical, I have put this into practice in several congregations, bringing each to a degree of relevancy. I have also shared it with other colleagues and congregations so they could do the same.

This book is targeted at pastors, congregational leaders, and any member passionate about being part of a relevant, missional congregation. For those pastors or leaders just starting in a new church (or churches) or wanting to jump-start ministry in the church they currently lead, I am hopeful this book will help guide your congregation to relevance. It will take time, discipline, consistency, and much prayer. Above all, it will take the divine leading of the Holy Spirit within your life, the life of the congregational leaders, and ultimately each person within the congregation you currently lead or will lead in the future.

It can be done! What a difference when your congregation moves from surviving to thriving, ultimately becoming relevant.

---

[10] Thom and Joani Schultz, *Why Nobody Wants to Go to Church Anymore* (Loveland: Group, 2013), 27

1

SPIRITUAL LEADERSHIP

There are numerous books written on leadership, so this chapter is not trying to write a new one. Many authors on leadership have given examples of great leaders, methods to become a great leader, and the desired characteristics of a leader. Most recently, the differences between leadership in business and the church have become less significant, with the concept of servant-leadership becoming increasingly popular. Of course, the best and most accurate example of servant-leadership is Jesus, exemplified in John 13:1–17. While similarities between business and faith-based leadership exist, there is a call for a different type of leadership within the church. Authentic *spiritual* leadership that reflects Christ and pursues God wholeheartedly.

Of definitions on leadership offered during the past decades by prominent authors and leaders, one of the most significant for church leaders comes from Henry and Richard Blackaby in their timeless book *Spiritual Leadership*. "Spiritual leadership is moving people on to God's agenda."[11] I cannot think of a better definition for pastors and leaders within the faith context. We often find leaders who led congregations on their personal agenda rather than God's. The results prove this: mediocrity, lack of spiritual influence, churches on the decline, and individuals' lives spiritually stagnant. Often these perceived great leaders become the focal point, and when they left or worse, failed morally, the church or organization suffered for it in the long term.

---

[11] Henry T. Blackaby and Richard Blackaby, *Spiritual Leadership* (Nashville: Broadman & Holman, 2010), 20

Spiritual Leadership

The Call to Spiritual Leadership

Being a leader is a privilege that is often taken for granted. When working within the church, or faith-based organization, it is a sacred call not to be taken lightly by those given the privilege of being selected by God for the task. The call to spiritual leadership comes through humans, but it originates with God. For whatever reason, which God alone knows, He selects certain men and women as His leaders with the desire they lead His people on His agenda. Most often, they are not the individuals we would choose (think Samuel and his reluctant selection of David), but God sees within the chosen individual the capacity for spiritual leadership.

True spiritual leaders are becoming more difficult to find in our times. William Sangster, a Methodist minister in the early twentieth century, stated, "The church is painfully in need of leaders. I wait to hear a voice, and no voice comes. I would rather listen than speak, but there is no clarion voice to listen to."[12] If this was the plaintive call almost a hundred years ago, what could we say about the need for spiritual leaders today in the twenty-first century?

We have numerous individuals within our churches today with the title of leader. This may be a named position, a self-designation, or one based on influence. But of the thousands of leaders we have, how many could be called true *spiritual* leaders? Churches, and other faith-based entities, cycle through leaders, hoping to find the one they need who can take their organization to the next level. They admire the perceived success of a leader's current or former church or organization, hoping they will duplicate it in their new position. These individuals being sought after are leaders, but are they *spiritual* leaders?

Which measurements are being used to mark a spiritual leader's success? Metrics are essential for evaluation within a congregation, but often spiritual leadership is not measured the same as the traditional indicators of success, such as financial contributions, increased attendance and membership, baptisms, community awareness, and status. I am confident a spiritual leader's measurements, while they may include some or all the former, go deeper, as they involve relevancy, impact, and influence.

How many lives have been affected and influenced? If one were able to measure the individuals within the congregation and community the spiritual

---

[12] Quoted by Paul E. Sangster, *Doctor Sangster* (London: Epworth), 1962

leader has been leading, what would be the results regarding discipleship and spiritual growth? Would these individuals be able to say they look more like Jesus today than they did a year ago? Could they say they have met Jesus personally through the influence of the leader? On the continuum[13] of an atheist on the far left (-10) to a person ready for translation on the far right (+10), has the leader brought people closer to Christ through their example, work, and other leadership influences? Are these leaders moving the congregation to a deeper relationship with God, further spiritual growth, and a desire to share God with others?

Are these leaders influencing others outside their sphere of leadership responsibility? Do those in the community respect and consider the voice of the spiritual leader? When considering a person's leadership capabilities and future potential, these are rarely measured, rarely asked about, and often ignored by denominational leaders and congregations in search of their next leader. When measuring a leader versus a *spiritual* leader, remember this: one is vast; the other is deep. Which one would you build the future of a congregation or faith-based organization upon? Your choice will dictate the future outcomes.

The Need for Spiritual Leaders

Lee Iacocca, "father" of the Ford Mustang and well-known former CEO of the Chrysler Corporation in the 1980s, published his book in 2007 with the provocative title *Where Have All the Leaders Gone?* Iacocca recognized that leaders who made a difference were lacking in the business and political world and asked for a new generation of leaders to step up and lead. He asked passionately, "Where are the curious, creative communicators? Where are the people of character, courage, conviction, competence, and common sense?"[14] I echo his call with a twist; where have all the leaders with these characteristics, who are also *spiritual* leaders, gone? There are those men and women working in quiet confidence, often unnoticed by their denominational leaders and other interested organizations, who are making a difference in people's lives by their spiritual leadership. Yet there is still an urgent need for

---

[13] As created by Bill Bright, founder of Campus Crusaders for Christ.
[14] Lee Iacocca, with Catherine Whitney, *Where Have All the Leaders Gone?* (New York: Scribner, 2007), 12

Spiritual Leadership

more spiritual leaders to step forward, recognized as called by God for this time and place.

J. Oswald Sanders's determined need for "authoritative, spiritual, and sacrificial" leaders is ever present. "Authoritative, because people desire reliable leaders who know where they are going and are confident of getting there. Spiritual, because without a strong relationship with God even the most attractive and competent person cannot lead people to God. Sacrificial, because this trait follows the model of Jesus, who gave Himself for the whole world and who calls us to follow in His step."[15]

These individuals who exemplify the spiritual leadership qualities Sanders speaks of are not trained by people but by the Holy Spirit. Their leadership is cultivated through the years as their relationship with God matures and deepens. Every leader's journey is different and unique, just as each person is unique. "In the life of faith, each person discovers all the elements of a unique and original adventure. We are prevented from following in one another's footsteps and are called to an incomparable associate with Christ," according to Eugene Peterson.[16] It is a slow journey, never accomplished overnight, but daily, nonetheless.

As E. M. Bounds observed, "It takes twenty years to make the sermon because it takes twenty years to make the man."[17] Substitute another task for "sermon," and the truth of that statement still applies. We need cultivated, committed spiritual leaders more than ever. We will find them in many places when we begin to use the right metrics to prove they exist and are doing their chosen work, fruits of an abundant and abiding relationship with God.

Leadership in Action

I have been blessed with meeting numerous leaders in my ministry, many of whom exemplified authentic spiritual leadership. One who fits the criteria of Sanders stands out above the rest. In 2010, my denominational leaders suggested that I join the Community Praise Center (CPC) staff in Alexandria, Virginia, where Henry Wright, PhD, was senior pastor. I wasn't happy about the new assignment, but a friend of mine, a very qualified attorney, suggested it may be an opportunity to learn from one of the finest in the denomination,

---

[15] J. Oswald Sanders, *Spiritual Leadership* (Chicago: Moody, 2007), 18
[16] As quoted by Will Mancini, *Church Unique* (San Francisco: Josses-Bass, 2008), 5
[17] E.M. Bounds, *E.M. Bounds on Prayer* (New Kensington: Whitaker House), 468

something akin to my friend working and learning directly from a Supreme Court justice. Why would any lawyer turn that down? Why should I turn down this opportunity to learn from a seasoned and respected leader?

I prayed about it and took on my new assignment with the personal commitment to shut my mouth, open my ears, and soak up everything I could from this experienced minister. When I arrived at CPC, Henry Wright had already served forty-eight years of ministry and eighteen years at CPC. When he first arrived at CPC, his core membership consisted of twenty-one people, and the church owed thousands of dollars to their denominational conference.

The church held a twenty-year celebration of Henry Wright's ministry at CPC two years after my arrival. In the brief slideshow honoring his time as senior pastor for the past twenty years, it was noted that the congregation had grown from those 21 members to more than 1,200 at the current time. A new church had been planted with greater than six hundred members, and another church plant was being established. Wright's ministry was successful by every metric, but the proof was in lives touched.

Henry Wright led a relevant congregation. He did it with an authoritative voice (not to be confused with loud) in the pulpit and out, leading others with humility, demonstrating in public what he cultivated in private, a deep and abiding relationship with Christ. Discipleship was crucial to Wright, walking with people on their spiritual journeys and sharing God with others. The congregation was relevant and mission-focused and excelled in many ways due to Wright's spiritual leadership. I witnessed an actual exhibition of God-chosen *spiritual* leadership in action.

Filling the Need

Perhaps you are a true spiritual leader. Maybe you would not consider yourself one yet, but desire to be. I quote Sanders once more: "Every generation faces the stringent demands of spiritual leadership, and most, unfortunately, turn away. But God welcomes the few who come forward to serve."[18] Do you earnestly desire to answer the call to spiritual leadership or strengthen and nurture your spiritual leadership? We need you! The church needs you, and your congregation or faith-based organization needs you!

---

[18] J. Oswald Sanders, *Spiritual Leadership* (Chicago: Moody, 2007), 18

Spiritual Leadership

Spiritual leadership is not an overnight transformation but comes from a daily intentional surrender and submission to God's call and purposes. He called, He will lead and provide.

Spiritual leaders engage in an abiding relationship with God, engage lives around them, and lead relevant congregations (or faith-based organizations). We need these spiritual leaders more than ever. God has called you to be more than just a leader; He is calling you to be a *spiritual* leader.

The question remains, will you accept the call?

2

DO-RE-MI

Perhaps Fräulein Maria was on to something. Waltzing around pre-WWII Salzburg, Austria, with Captain von Trapp's children, Maria, portrayed by actress Julia Andrews in *The Sound of Music*, wanted to teach the children how to sing for the Captain, their father. The children asked a logical question, "But how?" Maria's response became one of the most loved songs in the classic musical, *The Sound of Music*. "Let's start at the very beginning," Maria sang, "a very good place to start ... When you sing you begin with Do-re-mi." And soon she began to sing, "Doe, a deer, a female deer ..."[19] The rest is musical and cinematic history. As Maria belted out, it starts with the basics, or fundamentals, and from there, one can create just about anything.

I have long been fascinated by coaches who create winning teams from seemingly average players. I admire these five coaches: John Wooden, Pat Summit, Nick Saban, Vince Lombardi, and Bill Belichick. These are five coaches from the collegiate and pro levels who created sports dynasties. Between these five coaches, thirty-six championships have been achieved in their respective sports. Wooden won ten titles coaching the UCLA Bruins men's basketball team, including seven in a row from 1967 to 1973. Pat Summit coached the Tennessee Lady Vols women's basketball team to thirty-one NCAA tournaments, capturing eight NCAA titles. Nick Saban began coaching the Crimson Tide (University of Alabama) in 2007, leading them to six championships in fifteen seasons and a

---

[19] *The Sound of Music*, 57:14 - 1:02:50

win-loss record of 183-25 in the same period. These three coaches raised the bar in college sports.

Vince Lombardi became head coach of the NFL's moribund Green Bay Packers in 1959. He took the Packers from a 1-10-1 season before he arrived, to a championship in 1961. The Packers won five titles from 1961 to 1967, including the first two Super Bowls. Lombardi's name lives on with the Lombardi Trophy presented to each year's Super Bowl Champion. Love him or loathe him, head coach Bill Belichick has led the New England Patriots to an unheard-of six Super Bowl wins, in nine appearances, over 21 seasons. His remarkable run began in 2001, and as he is still the head coach of the New England Patriots as of this writing who knows how much more history will be written within the NFL books from his team.

These head coaches, who led their teams to multiple championships, had one thing in common; they emphasized fundamentals. Each placed an extreme value and purpose on the fundamentals from training camp to the championship game. Listen to winning coaches and how they took their team back to the fundamentals, resulting in a championship. Listen to losing coaches; they will say there is a need to get their team back to the fundamentals. Belichick and Saban call it "The Process." Drilling into their players to focus on "The Process," they both know desired outcomes will result.

As related by David Maraniss in his biography of Vince Lombardi, *When Pride Still Mattered*, Coach Lombardi began each training camp the same way. "Gentleman," he said, holding a pigskin in his right hand, "this is a football."[20] Why? Maraniss explains, "He began a tradition of starting from scratch, assuming that players were blank slates who carried over no knowledge from the year before. He reviewed the fundamentals of blocking and tackling, the basic plays, how to read the playbook."[21] Many of these were the same players who had been on the Packers team the year before. They created terrific and often improvised plays, winning championships and setting the field on fire with their playmaking skills. Lombardi never wanted them to forget that football fundamentals are where it all begins, no matter how successful they might become.

John Wooden coached some of the most talented NCAA and future NBA

---

[20] David Maraniss, *When Pride Still Mattered: A Life of Vince Lombardi* (New York: Simon & Shuster, 1999), 274

[21] Maraniss, 274

players during his time at UCLA. Bill Walton, Walt Hazzard, Sidney Wicks, and Kareem Abdul-Jabbar top the list, each with incredible ball-handling skills, bringing showtime to L.A. before the Lakers did. Yet, for all their collective skills John Wooden continually preached to them, and every other player who walked into practice, fundamentals mattered most. He preferred two-handed passes to the flashy one-hand, behind-the-back pass only because he believed that fundamentals would never change, even if style did. Whatever his players would do on the court during games, he brought them back to fundamentals every practice. He knew the fundamentals allowed them to be creative and flash their ball-handling skills more effectively, leading to even more championships. His stress on fundamentals led him to teach every player, at the beginning of every training camp, how to put their socks on correctly to avoid blisters and time off the court that this minor injury would guarantee.

I have risked the tedium (and the ire of those who had their favorite team beat by one of the coaches written about) of stressing the importance of fundamentals for a reason. As leaders, many of us are tempted to bypass the worn path of fundamentals for modern methods and practices we are told will change the leadership success game and make the difference. Trends and techniques come and go, but fundamentals never will. The same is valid for fundamental leadership and best practices, thus the purpose of this book, how to effectively lead a congregation to relevancy.

Leaders often go to conferences, listen to podcasts, read books, and visit the next thing in leadership to discover what is new and how to raise their measurable success rates. I have found the same applies in the business world, so leaders within the spiritual field are not alone in their thinking. Many theories and practices are championed as something new, but when all is tried, the fundamentals still bring success. Different styles and methods can increase relevancy due to culture or demographics, but not at the expense of fundamentals.

Perhaps you disagree. Let me press my point just a bit further. I love automobiles! Over the past 120+ years of automotive history the style of the automobile has changed dramatically, reflecting the time and design cues of the era. What has not changed? Each one has an engine, transmission, and four wheels which have (almost) existed since the automobile was created. The body styles, capabilities, and number of options and luxury may have changed, but the fundamental design of operation never will. This is not unlike the church which has changed shape drastically since launched by Jesus through the disciples in the first century. Yet for all the changes over two millennia, the fundamental message is still the same, as is the process for relevance.

I would like to challenge you to consider the value of fundamentals in your personal spiritual growth and leadership within the congregation or organization you serve. The *Congregation Development Model*, which we are ready to explore, is based on fundamentals. There are twenty-one blocks to the development model, each representing a fundamental idea. How you decide to implement them in your congregation's context will look different. I am giving you the chassis with four wheels, an engine, and a transmission; you decide what the body style on the chassis will look like. Please remember this as you proceed; times and fads will change, and the wind will always blow something new in, but fundamentals will never change.

> *The basketball still goes in the net.*

> *The football still crosses the goal line.*

> *God still changes lives through relevant congregations.*

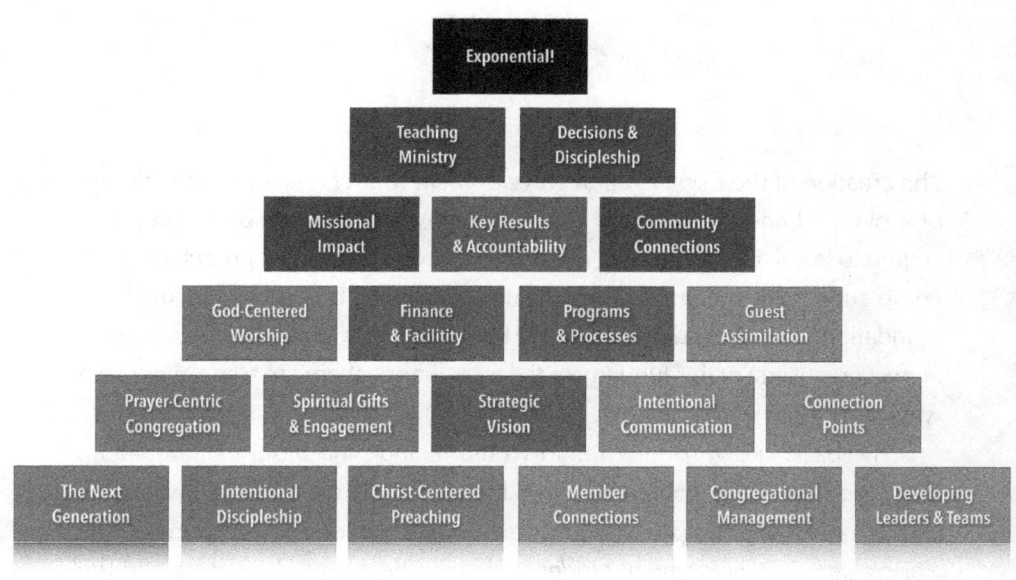

This graphic is available as a full-color download in letter-size format, or poster format, by visiting www.therelevanctcongregation.com. It may be reproduced for congregational use.

3

THE MODEL

The creation of the *Congregation Development Model* is based on the design of a pyramid and conceptually on the John Wooden *Pyramid of Success*. A system to build a long-standing pyramid requires a specific approach to reach completion. The pinnacle of a pyramid can never be completed until the foundation, interior, and sides are fully built and ready to solidify the pinnacle. However, outside of this fundamental design theory, there are some alternative ways a pyramid could be built.

The basic design of a pyramid would include the base, or foundation, laid first, then slowly completing level by level until construction reaches the peak. Considering this primary construction method, one could approach the *Congregation Development Model* similarly. There would be a start in the middle, then working outward, fully completing the development foundation before moving to the next level. The next level would continue from the center, again working towards the edges, moving up to the completed pinnacle.

Another alternative is to begin in the middle by creating a smaller pyramid, then edging out one fundamental block and up, forming an interior peak before starting the process again and finally reaching completion. And lest you think a pyramid cannot be built this way, through this model or in actuality, French architect Jean-Pierre Houdin would disagree.[22] Another option is to begin towards one side or the other, as the needs of the process dictate. This

---

[22] Reuters, *Great Pyramid Was Built Inside Out*, 2007 (https://www.reuters.com/article/us-egypt-pyramid/great-pyramid-was-built-inside-out-frenchman-says-idUSL3039256920070330), Accessed June 2, 2022

is irregular, yet possible, and the same goal is accomplished, completing the pinnacle and a finished pyramid design.

Why the Order Matters

As noted in the introduction, this *Congregation Development Model* has been seven years in the making, tweaked with experience, observation, and conversations with numerous leaders. It assumes a starting point and builds from that point to full completion. It works best for leaders who have accepted a call into a new congregation, but it can also work for leaders who want to revive their current field of ministry. A pastor coming into a recent call could establish this model as their road map for the next one to three years, using these fundamentals to guide success and relevancy. It is not impossible, but it is difficult, for a pastor to hit the reset button of their current congregation and instill this model as a guide, or even harder, graft it into what they already have in place. Not impossible, but not easy either. Being the positive leader I am, I would tackle anything if I knew the Holy Spirit was guiding me through it.

The model is developed into four specific areas: *spiritual* (green), *relational* (orange), *practicable* (blue), and *missional* (red). Starting from the middle on the foundation level, as designed, one immediately straddles the spiritual and relational components and quickly adds the practicable element. Slowly all three are built up until they sustain the missional role a congregation is ready to assume. All four areas are essential, but the first two, *spiritual* and *relational*, might be the most vital to begin the work of establishing a relevant congregation.

Because I sometimes like to break the predictable rules, I have tried to lead a congregation on a different path to success, creating shortcuts to the desired result. In doing so, I learned the hard way that there is a reason why a builder doesn't put the roof on the house first. I echo Coach Saban's term, "The Process," recognizing there is a natural way to complete this model, bringing sustained success. You may have previously attempted shortcuts to success within your congregation. If so, you would likely agree the results have not been good. Some things just can't be achieved with shortcuts.

The Model

Not All or Nothing

While the development model works best through a holistic approach, building from the base to the pinnacle, please don't dismiss all the fundamentals if my approach isn't suitable for you or the congregation you lead. These fundamentals included are all, in my opinion, needed within congregations today. Yes, some of these fundamentals become more effective by other fundamentals successfully implemented first. As I have stated previously, the order and process of the fundamentals matter, and have been researched, as well as implemented in congregations I have pastored, to determine their positioning and ultimate success. However, even if the model does not seem to fit for you, I would urge you not to dismiss all the fundamentals, and consider each as useful within a congregation, even if the model isn't implemented.

It has been a long journey to this book, and I am excited to take leaders like you through this model. I will do so by sketching out the basics and providing the purpose and goal for each fundamental building block, allowing you to use your local context, culture, and creativity to bring each to fruition. I have seen what happens when this model is worked through with diligence, prayer, and ultimately the leading of the Holy Spirit. I am confident it will do the same for you and your congregation.

4

THE RIGHT START

A pastor arrives at their new congregation. The excitement of the interview, subsequent move, and a fresh beginning have them ready to go. So many possibilities, so many opportunities. What should be done first? I have seen pastors seek to make their mark the first weekend in their congregation by moving an article of furniture or decoration off the platform. A quick redesign of the bulletin does the trick too. Not so subtle ways to let the congregation know the old pastor is gone and a new pastor is here to lead. They've been warned!

Maybe there is a better way. Checking out the *Congregation Development Model*, you will find two fundamental blocks to the left and right of the center on the base: *Christ-Centered Preaching* and *Member Connections*. One is public, the other private. If a pastor were to ask me what to do first, *Christ-Centered Preaching* or *Member Connections*, my resounding answer would be yes, each running in parallel with the other, public and private impact joined together.

Power of Preaching

Which one is of most value? Which will make the immediate difference? If forced to answer that burning question, I lean toward Christ-centered preaching. Nothing beats a first impression, and many will come to hear the new preacher within their first few weeks in the pulpit. The first month of sermons in a new congregation, or one chosen to revitalize, are the most crucial ones the pastor will preach. They set the tone for their tenure and bring many listeners to a decision as to whether they will stay in the congregation moving forward or leave to join another faith community.

I had been in my one congregation for close to a year when I got into a specific conversation with an elder. He related a perspective that has stuck with me since. Based on my first sermon, he gained insight into my relationship with God, my ministry passions, and how I would lead the congregation forward. I had to think back to what I preached about which made an impression on his mind. There was an increased realization on my part as to the importance of the first sermons preached by the pastor in a new congregation or purposefully revitalizing congregation. The question then remains: if these sermons are of such significant value, what are you called to preach?

I recommend to all pastors and lay preachers the chapter "The Sermon Likely to Win Souls" from Charles Spurgeon's book, *The Soul Winner*. "Preach Jesus, brethren," he writes, "always and everywhere, and every time you preach, be sure to have much of Jesus Christ in the sermon." More than a century later, it is still wise counsel for the preacher to consider. Those listening get enough political commentary, opinion, and secular worldview without the preacher giving theirs from the pulpit. What the listener needs is Jesus now and forever preached. No matter the passage from the Word of God, preached "In season and in-out" (2 Timothy 4:2), your subject should center on, as does the Bible, Jesus. It will be contextual, no doubt, and fit the audience you are preaching to. Yet it will, and must, center on Jesus.

The power in preaching is the Subject preached. It is the current condition of humans in relationship to Jesus. It determines the greatest need for preaching today. The great British preacher, D. Martyn Lloyd-Jones wrote, "I mean that the moment you consider man's real need, and also the nature of the salvation announced and proclaimed in the Scriptures, you are driven to the conclusion that the primary task of the church is to preach and proclaim this, to show man's real need, and to show the only remedy, the only cure for it."[23] That cure, as we know, is Jesus.

---

[23] D. Martyn Lloyd-Jones, *Preaching and Preachers* (Grand Rapids: Zondervan Publishing House, 1972), 26

Preaching as Priority

If in the past you have not spent the needed hours of preparation for sermons, there is never a better time to adjust your schedule. In addition, prayer must run parallel within the preacher, for powerful prayers in fact make equally powerful sermons. Never underestimate what prayer and preaching do for each other, and in the ministry of a pastor or congregational leader selected to preach. "Prayer freshens the heart of the preacher, keeps it in tune with God and in sympathy with the people. It lifts his ministry out of the chilly air of a profession, revitalizes routine, and moves every wheel with the ease and power of a divine anointing."[24]

It is a tendency on our part as pastors and congregational leaders to select topics that are meaningful to us personally or allow us to continue to ride our favorite hobby horse. The best, and most challenging sermons to prepare, have come to me as a result of praying intently for God to reveal what I should be preaching to the congregation. While a pastor knows their congregation members from the surface, only the Holy Spirit knows what is deep within the people, and what they need to hear at a given time or place. When coming into a new congregation the most important prayer will be, "God, what do they need to hear from You, through me?"

I really believe the most significant influence of a pastor is from the pulpit. Don't neglect the time needed to prepare sermons, and the prayers that lead up to those sermons, as well as needed while preparing them. I have been surprised often the direction the Holy Spirit will take a sermon when I diligently seek wisdom and insight into what I will be sharing on a given weekend. Every week is an opportunity for people to see God through the lens of your sermon. What will they see in you, what will they hear through you? "Talking to men for God is a great thing ..."[25] Use it wisely.

I urge you to reconsider the importance of the pulpit if you have not made preaching a priority to this point. If preaching isn't your best skill, consider improving it. If delivery and presentation don't come easy for you, find a course that can help you. Also, don't neglect the power of presentation through your PowerPoint or Keynote slides. I challenge you to take your preaching to another level, and the increase it will bring to the congregation—not to be

---

[24] E.M. Bounds, *E.M. Bounds on Prayer* (Grand Rapids: Whitaker House, 2012), 478
[25] *Bounds*, 479

The Right Start

done to make you look better, but that you may be an effective vessel through whom the Holy Spirit flows. If possible, do all of this before starting your new assignment. If you are already within a congregation, make the adjustments on the fly or take a sabbatical to insert the needed changes.

As admonished so succinctly by Michael Fabarez, "We must never underestimate, or by our tone or manner antiquate, the timeless power of biblical preaching. By it, God transforms His people ..."[26] Preaching will have its place in every congregation, and every pastor and/or spiritual leader has a sacred duty to represent God well in the pulpit and through the sermons preached.

In a dry and dusty time and place, where people are hungering for God, present the Living Water, the Bread of Life, and the Light, which no darkness of this world can overcome. The first sermon should invite the listener to join you in seeking God, taking His promise as yours and theirs; "If you seek Me, you will find Me, if you seek Me with all of your heart." Jeremiah 29:13. The first sermon, or series of sermons, doesn't need to declare there is a new pastor in town, but that Jesus Christ is still Lord of this congregation, and He has called you to be His chosen messenger to the congregation.

The Power of Presence

While preaching Christ-centered sermons each week, there may be no better alternative use of time than engaging members in personal visits. Immediately! It has become increasingly rare to find pastors willing to visit with their congregants. I've had numerous members in the past tell me that in ten, twenty, and even thirty years of church membership, they never had a pastor cross their threshold just to spend time getting acquainted with them! I am convinced, no, convicted; there is no better way to build trust within the congregation and propel it forward quickly to becoming relevant.

Several years ago, I was preparing to transition from associate pastor for Community Praise Church to a new position as lead pastor in another congregation. As I was preparing to make a move and embark on a new adventure, I conversed with one of my mentors. In previous conversations, he had impressed on my mind the value of visits, but this time on the phone, he

---

[26] Michael Fabarez, *Preaching that Changes Lives* (Nashville: Thomas Nelson, 2002), 6

drove the point home. Visit, visit, visit, and watch the difference those visits make. He spoke from several decades of senior pastoral experience and knew firsthand the benefits of pastoral visits. He made such an indelible impression on me during that conversation that I made a personal commitment to put visits as a priority in my next assignment. Within a few days, I worked with my new administrative assistant to set up the scheduling blocks to be presented the first weekend I would be with the new congregation.

On the first weekend I preached, all attendees that day were invited to schedule a pastoral visit. The church's foyer had a table with three weeks of scheduling blocks available to sign up for. Each block was 1.5 hours long. On days when I chose to do multiple visits, there were 30-minute travel intervals between them. I asked members to consider scheduling close in proximity to other members who had already signed up or work with those close to them in location when scheduling their appointments. Quickly the three weeks filled up. The day following my first appearance in the pulpit and as the congregation's pastor, I began visiting members who had signed up. They were simple visits. I wanted to know three things. First, tell me about you personally and your spiritual journey. Second, what do you love about your church? Lastly, if you could change anything about your church, what would it be? I learned other things about my members, but these were the three core questions I wanted to be answered each time.

Something unique immediately began to take place. First, members saw the pastoral visits were actual, for they could see the scheduling blocks others were filling out. Within a couple of weeks, word got around that they had a "visiting pastor," something the congregation hadn't been blessed with in quite some time. Members had fun with the visits too, and so did some visitors. I committed to meeting people wherever they chose. Home, church office, Starbucks, Panera Bread, the park, or (almost) any place of their choosing. I got taken out to eat a few times, met in my office for a few, and walked with others, but I had most of my ninety-minute visits within the homes of my congregants.

Within 100 days of arriving, I visited thirty-four families! I cannot begin to explain the impact of each visit. The trust and friendships initiated in the first three months paid maximum dividends over the next eighteen months in the life and relevancy of the congregation. Friendships formed, and bonds of trust were created. I gave equal attention to the children and youth within

The Right Start

the congregation as well, often attending games they played in, one-on-one conversations just hanging out at the church, and speaking to them directly during home visits.

Let me add something here regarding home visits, versus meeting anywhere else. There is much to be learned by observation when you're able to meet your congregant within their home. You learn about immediate and extended family through photos and memories around the home. Hobbies and interests are observed, and often the member will give a demonstration or explain further why they enjoy particular interests. You also learn more about their personal preferences and the reasons for them. I have found people are the most comfortable being on their own "turf," and are more transparent in conversation because of it. I am finding lately that many prefer not to have a home visit, but if your members or guests will allow it, I recommend it.

Loving the Sheep

Perhaps the greatest reward from the pastoral visits was the love I developed for my members. I began to care deeply for them; not seeing them as objects used to accomplish my success, but as individuals God called me to serve. It came more rapidly than expected, within months, rather than years. It influenced interactions, conversations, board meetings, preaching, and my personal prayer life. It is difficult to be upset with a member when they become part of your private pastoral prayers! When disagreements arose, I dealt more graciously with individuals, and they responded the same, for they knew their pastor cared enough to visit them, learn about them, and love them sincerely. I was also transparent and authentic privately and from the pulpit, which developed another dimension of ministry that was entirely unexpected.

The apostle Peter expressed well the role of the spiritual leader; "Here's my concern: that you care for God's flock with all the diligence of a shepherd. Not because you must, but because you want to please God. Not calculating what you can get out of it but acting spontaneously. Not bossily telling others what to do, but tenderly showing them the way." 2 Peter 5:2,3; *The Message*. This is the calling of a spiritual leader, and one many members of a congregation have rarely seen from their pastor or leaders but most certainly would like to. As spiritual leaders, we may be called to do many things for God, but loving His people is the most important one of all.

Make visits and connections with members a priority. Even when you have done initial visits when you arrive, consider follow-up ones as ministry progresses over the next months and years in the congregation. A brief visit, and follow-up phone calls, with the intent to pray with a member, showing that you care, is more valuable than anything else a pastor can do. This simple effort makes the sermon more personal each week and builds deep abiding relationships with members that allow you to join their journey of discipleship.

The Best First Steps

Preach original, Christ-centered sermons each week, visit members, and begin to express God's vision for the congregation: those are the best first steps any pastor or lay leader could pursue. Make these fundamentals a priority, even at the expense of setting up your office, rearranging the platform, or changing the font in the bulletin. The congregation will quickly know what matters most to you by your priorities. They will soon have no doubt that preaching Jesus, loving people, and moving forward with God's agenda is a leadership priority that will lead the congregation to a new destination: relevance.

5

Strategic Vision

~

1843 began the "Great Emigration," the trek of thousands of people each year on the Oregon Trail seeking a better life. They left the known of the eastern United States for the unknown of the West, driven by a vision of more than they currently had. The Pacific Ocean, the promise of abundant crops on land available for those willing to take the perilous journey. Trail guides organized groups each winter, ready to leave Independence, Missouri, by April or May to complete the trip west before winter set in. Each guide needed to plan strategically, cast a vision, communicate clearly, and compel people with a clear purpose for their journey.

The trail guide monitored each day's progress, urging settlers to pick up the pace or travel an extra hour in a day if needed. When people wanted to turn back, complained, or grew weary, the trail guide would describe the destination and what to expect when they got there. Casting vision, communicating purpose, measuring the journey, and leading people on to better than they came from, the trail guide kept people focused and pressing forward. It isn't unlike what a leader is called to do within a congregation or faith-based organization today. More importantly, it is another part of spiritual leadership you have been called to.

Indeed, there have been times when you could relate to the 19th Century trail guide keeping a large group of settlers motivated and moving in the right direction. As leaders within the congregation, there are always those who want to maintain the status quo, go back to what was or are the first ones to speak up when obstacles present themselves. A measurable, well-communicated strategic vision is essential to keeping your congregation united and progressing to relevancy. Authors Kouzes and Posner of *The Truth About Leadership* explain why; "Throughout human history people have risked life, security, and wealth for something that is greater than themselves. People want a chance to take part in something meaningful and important."[27] A compelling vision of a relevant congregation is a powerful force for meaning and creating positive changes. Without it, there is wandering in circles, creating confusion. "When people can't see what God is up to, they stumble all over themselves." Proverbs 29:18, *The Message*.

Day One Vision-Casting

Whether preaching an original sermon or sermon series for the new congregation, or scheduling visits with those who desire them (and I often asked for the visit, not waiting to be invited), the first several weeks are crucial to lay out God's vision and future for the congregation you serve. A compelling vision provides energy, hope, dependence on God, focus, and defined purpose. This invites the fundamental of *Strategic Vision* to come into play in the development model. I do not think it is necessary to craft a unique vision for each congregation in the United States when Jesus has given us an idea of what every relevant congregation should look like. Sharing a strategic vision through sermons and visits can be broad and biblical. Ultimately, every vision for the congregation should center on Christ's purpose and promise for His congregation within their context.

Talking about the strategic vision component so quickly from the pulpit and with people privately is a positive that should not be ignored. People are stirred to something better and may engage sooner in the outcomes and stories envisioned; this provides new energy. Another valuable insight is listening to people respond in conversation when asked what they would change about their church if they could. Some just tell you what they would change, and others offer solutions to facilitate the desired change; this provides hope. The ones that offer solutions are potential candidates for a Strategic Vision Team you will want to form within the next six months by permission of your

---

[27] James M. Kouzes & Barry Z. Posner, *The Truth About Leadership* (San Francisco: Jossey-Bass, 2010),66

Strategic Vision

leadership team or board, depending on your congregation's structure. These individuals will help you provide the focus needed within the congregation.

It can be quite tempting to wait to vision-cast with your leadership teams and congregation until after you have been there a while. But why? As stated already, the vision for every congregation is to be healthy, relevant and make a spiritual impact on individuals, done so within the context of the congregation's placement. This is the *ekklēsia* Jesus built, one the first-century apostles and disciples moved forward on. As a spiritual leader tuned in to God's agenda, you are equipped by the Holy Spirit to cast a vision within the church even before you take on the task!

So rarely are members of a congregation exposed to a leader who communicates a compelling vision. They quickly get excited about the possibilities. They begin to sense God's movement as never before and a new dependence on Him, which increases faith. Some will jump right in and line up with the vision. Others dig in their heels and resist coming changes. However, if vision is shared from the beginning in sermons and visits, you will minimize the resistance and strengthen the will of those ready to push forward to a better future. You also have an opportunity to see the potential resistance points relatively quickly.

Leading with a Compelling Vision

Nehemiah is one of my favorite leaders in the Old Testament. He felt deep empathy for his fellow Jews who had returned from captivity to Jerusalem (Nehemiah 1:4). He answered God's call to lead the rebuilding of Jerusalem's walls (2:4,12), assessed the situation upon his arrival (2:11-16), shared a compelling vision immediately (2:17), and led God's people on God's agenda (2:20). The people responded emphatically, "Let us arise and build!" (18). As every leader knows, however, obstacles always arise, even with the best vision.

There were doubters. The ones that find every reason why something cannot be done. Sanballat mocked the Jews who undertook the task, "What are these feeble Jews doing? Are they going to restore it for themselves? Can they offer sacrifices? Can they finish in a day? Can they revive the stones from the dusty rubble even the burned ones?" (4:2) Tobiah, not to be outdone, jumped in, "Even what they are building—if a fox should jump on it, he would break their stone wall down!" (4:3)

When progress on the walls continued, those opposed went from doubting to despising, looking for ways to disrupt the progress (4:8). Nehemiah had to remind those involved in the work that this was God's vision and agenda, and He would see it through (4:14). He purposefully recast vision, reminded the people of their purpose, and encouraged people to move forward even with the mounting obstacles.

The most crucial part, Nehemiah was there with every stone placed on the walls (5:16). Present each day to allow the people to see the vision in action. Nehemiah had to remind the people of the purpose and desired outcome halfway through the project. The wall would be completed within fifty-two days, and twenty-six days into the rebuild the vision was recast. Like Nehemiah, a leader must lead to the vision by their words and actions, reminding people consistently while clarifying God's agenda and ultimate vision for His congregation. A vision that becomes a reality is often spoken of and acted upon intentionally.

A compelling vision will take a congregation further than any other tool within the leader's toolkit. The most compelling vision is not what you believe the future should be but what God has shown them, through you, it to be. There is a biblical basis for this vision and enough stories along the journey to prove it is the preferred future God is leading towards. You must demonstrate to the congregation that the vision is authentic and compelling by being involved personally and communicating consistently in the pulpit and privately.

Andy Stanley emphatically writes, "When it comes to making your vision stick, here is the most important thing to remember: You are responsible. It is the leader's responsibility to ensure that people understand and embrace the organization's vision."[28] This is a significant responsibility, but the leader has the highest credibility to cast the vision for the congregation.

The Partnership of Strategy and Vision

I am a firm believer in strategic planning. So much so that I completed my MBA with an emphasis on non-profits with a focus on strategy and

---

[28] Andy Stanley, *Making Vision Stick* (Grand Rapids: Zondervan, 2007), 17

development for organizations. I have worked with various congregations and schools to help them find a strategic way forward and have seen positive results. A well-designed strategic plan should begin to show measurable results within six months. Furthermore, a clear strategy helps define the church's purpose and allows leaders to make decisions based on the desired outcome of the strategic vision. In working with most congregations, there are many common initiatives and metrics, as each congregation is ultimately called to the same result by God. Often, components reflect a congregation's challenges, like facility issues, specifics in various ministries or community context.

For reasons I have yet to fully explain, most congregational leaders are reluctant to consider a strategic plan or dismiss it outright. Many don't even fully grasp the idea of a vision or its importance. Author and consultant Will Mancini relates his experience with pastors, "What goes through the minds of most pastors I meet? They affirm that vision is important, but they lack clarity for what it really looks like. Strategic planning is nowhere on their radar."[29] This corresponds with many I have met. Yet, there is another reality for congregations that have engaged in strategic planning, one Mancini follows up on, "Churches either had an outdated strategic plan, with too much information that paralyzed action ... or they had photocopied another church's vision without much thought and, therefore, without adequate meaning or application."[30] With many pastors and leaders I have spoken to, strategic planning is considered laborious, unproductive and unnecessary. Thus, they do not wish even to consider it. This reality prevents most congregations from ever becoming truly relevant.

Without a plan to get there, a vision is just another great idea. It would be having a destination for a vacation, yet never following a map and directions to get there. I cannot reinforce my belief enough that vision and strategy go together every time. The right measurables help determine progress towards the vision and allow for celebration when set points are reached and allow for needed adjustments to be made when they are not. There are different strategic planning methods available, but the proper approach keeps the congregation focused, active, and does not exist unused on a hard drive or sit on a shelf.

---

[29] Will Mancini and Warren Bird, *God Dreams* (Nashville: Broadman & Holman Publishing, 2016), 9

[30] *Mancini and Bird*, 10

I do not know why more congregations won't embrace strategic planning. There is a fear for some that it may take them through change, and many resist change. There are congregations I have observed that still do today what they did twenty to thirty years ago. When speaking to leaders and members within the congregation, there is frustration that nothing has happened, and no forward progress is being made. I have no reason to wonder why that is when they tell me they never had a plan to get out of the rut of status quo. A well-thought-out, fully implemented strategic vision can take a congregation out of the wilderness of mediocrity to God's preferred future.

SVT: High-Powered Results

The **S**trategic **V**ision **T**eam harnesses the agenda God has called the church to and designated you to lead as a spiritual leader. The individuals who serve on this team should understand the community demographics, the congregation's demographics, including spiritual awareness and engagement, and establish the purpose, goals, and key initiatives necessary for the congregation to become increasingly relevant. A spiritual leader, leading people on God's agenda, already knows where to go and will use the Strategic Vision Team to map out how to get there. As stated in another chapter, work with the teams, so everyone owns it!

Before forming the Strategic Vision Team (by the way, the initials SVT were used by Ford for years for their modified cars that increased speed, handling, and their resulting fun factor), I ask a congregation to take a survey that gives insight into demographics of those who attend and are members. This is crucial when forming the team because it works more effectively to have a representation across key demographics. Ethnicity, age, and gender are the key factors; others may surface when the survey results come in. Having teenagers to retired folks on the team, with everyone in between, gives insight and understanding from differing generations. Varying ethnicities also provides an understanding of how diverse people think and feel about their congregation, worship, ministry, and more. Valuable insights are gained with a broad demographic representation, much is lost when this is neglected.

The team size may vary but should reflect the size of the congregation to some extent. Understand that the larger the team, the increasing difficulty to wield such a team. When inviting a person to the team, it is easy to ask those

Strategic Vision

already active within the church, but wisely avoid this trap. There are other valuable members in the congregation with incredible gifts and perspectives who will flourish and add value to the team. In one congregation, a Millennial attended who was not fully active in other areas of the church. Through prayer, they were invited to be on the team and lead the team. This individual excelled at the task and grew into other roles as a result. Be open-minded and aware of all your members, and you will begin to know whom to engage on the team. A significant dose of prayer, request for wisdom, and spiritual discernment is also necessary for adding the right people to the team.

The best team not only engages in initial strategic vision sessions but works in the coming months, and even years, to measure progress and adjust accordingly. Some may not be willing to make the time commitment for the long run but would be a strong person for the initial work. Add them regardless. It is often easier to find the long-term person when they see the Strategic Vision Team's results. There will be some in the congregation skeptical of the SVT's work and strategy overall. They will say it is not necessary within the context of the church. Give them a bible study on Nehemiah if these individuals voice objections and be patient. Let the future results speak for themselves.

Strategic, Purposeful, Relevant

A leader who embraces a strategic vision for their congregation is wise indeed. It allows decisions to be made, opportunities to be undertaken, and much more that would not occur outside the framework of the strategic vision. I have witnessed this occur in multiple churches. In one such congregation, major shifts began to take place in their missional attitude and worship service. When objections came up, as they always will when change begins to happen, the pastor pointed to the congregation's fully voted strategic vision, with its accompanying initiatives. There was nothing else the objectors could say. The congregation had previously voted, through the strategic vision, to make a move in a new direction of being relevant.

As the strategic vision moves forward, the leader begins to tell stories. Not just what has been but will be. They share stories of what the future will look like as God leads the congregation on to relevance. The results of a compelling strategic vision, with efforts to keep on track by evaluating metrics, and trimming the sails accordingly, are of more value than I can express here. I won't lead a congregation without a strategic vision, and a congregation likely won't become relevant without one either.

Please, never underestimate what vision means to your leadership. Ever. "Vision is the essential ingredient for successful leadership. There is no substitute. Without it, influence fades along with the crowds."[31] There might be some disagreement regarding this statement by Hyatt, but I believe most of it to be true. Vision, carried out with competent and compassionate action, referenced often verbally, drives a congregation to relevancy more completely than just about anything else a spiritual leader could do. You and I have both seen congregations that stagnate due to a lack of vision, and how difficult those congregations can be to revitalize once again.

Vision and purpose create change. Change is another conversation, but purposeful change is much easier to accomplish based on God's vision and agenda, fleshed out through the strategic vision. Now is the time to chart a new direction for your congregation with a compelling strategic vision for intentional ministry and missional growth. The effort will generate results that bring glory to God and create new outcomes for the congregation they never expected.

---

[31] Michael Hyatt, *The Vision Driven Leader* (Grand Rapids: Baker Books, 2020), 20

6

Congregational Management

The following fundamental, *Congregational Management*, moves towards the right from *Member Connections*. This fundamental practice is sorely lacking in most congregations yet urgently needed. This is using available tools to keep the congregation's information readily accessible and choosing a platform to organize this information for effective future use. Gone are the days of looking in the physical directory to find faces and information. Hard copies have been replaced by tools for keeping the most up-to-date information possible right at our fingertips, even on the go. While *Congregational Management* might seem like an administrative tool, it falls into the relational category, for it is the super-glue that keeps a congregation together. It is a valuable tool for every congregational leader and team.

Information is Relational

One of the best places to gather member and attendee information not readily available is during pastoral visits. A secondary gathering source is inviting members and attendees to complete a paper questionnaire or make it available online. Alternatively, smiling individuals could be made available with a tablet prior to services to have a brief conversation with people and gather the information verbally, inputted directly into the chosen platform.

Leading a Congregation to Relevance

There may be additional creative ways of gathering the information, but these three have worked quite well from experience.

What are the benefits of gathering information? Celebrating birthdays, anniversaries, graduations, life moments, and additional information such as spiritual gifts, talents, and medical needs, to name a few. This information provides essential knowledge within leadership and the members know their pastor and leaders care enough to ask and celebrate life points with them. It also aids in encouraging further engagement within the congregation as the relationships deepen. Initial information pieces to collect are:

- *Birthday*
- *Anniversary*
- *Children's grade level*
- *Marital Status*
- *Address*
- *Phone (Mobile & Landline)*
- *Email*
- *Alma Mater*
- *Hobbies & Interests*

Most members and attendees are willing to share this as a starting point, especially if they understand information is kept private and not shared wholesale across the congregation. It can depend on which platform is chosen, but members and attendees may also determine what information they would like available to the congregation at large and what remains private for only leaders and internal staff of the church to access. They also can add updated photos of themselves or their family which significantly assists in growing healthy bonds (and aids in name recall).

At the time of this writing, my favorite platform for congregation management is Planning Center Online[32] (from which I receive no financial benefit for endorsing). Their component for capturing this personal information is called *People*. The *People* component is free and a great tool to manage your congregation's information. It is web-based, secure, and provides many other tools that enhance ministry and build relationships. Once an individual is set up in Planning Center, they can access their data and update information,

---

[32] A free trial is available at https://www.planningcenter.com

Congregational Management

including a photo. Other systems are also available, one of the most prominent being Church Community Builder. Each platform has varying costs, but they are worth investing in for increased congregation growth and relationships.

The Benefits of Information

Once a congregation has the basic information set on the chosen platform, leaders can begin building stronger relationships with each member personally and as the congregation moves forward in growth and relevancy. It is easy to create ministry teams, small groups, participation and engagement notes, and event groups. Additionally, leadership can initiate processes, with the availability to schedule and communicate directly from the platform to individuals relating to each group or interest. As people ebb and flow from the congregation, their info is easily added and updated. As teams and groups change, it is similarly easy to add and remove names, accordingly, communicate efficiently, and share needed documents and information.

The best platforms allow for multiple aspects of information to be keyed in. College attended, medical concerns, social media presence, interests, and notes. I find all these extremely helpful, notes being my favorite. The saved notes can be private, allowing a pastor to input content from a personal visit or crucial conversations. An overview of any given individual provides all the information listed above immediately, except what is deemed private. Additionally, all communication avenues for an individual are listed, including leadership positions, and participation in small groups and teams. Extensive and practical, this repository is a powerful tool for all leaders, easily accessed on a computer, tablet, or smartphone.

Another best use of the platforms available is attendance for adults and children. For adults, it allows congregational leaders to spot trends when someone has not come for some time. It can be used in individual small groups, in study classes, or upon entrance of the building each week. How often has a church leader heard from a member they were not in attendance for quite some time, yet no one ever called or came to visit them. When guests arrive for the first time, it is easy to add them into the system, allowing processes to be implemented that create positive guest follow-up from chosen teams and leaders, including the pastor. For adults, taking attendance celebrates who is attending and provides a unique safety net of love and care for those missing.

There is a much-needed safety aspect on the children's level which is an incredible benefit. Set up check-ins for children when parents drop them off at classes, and the children cannot leave until the parent comes back to pick them up and the proper scans and identification are made. In one step, attendance is taken, and a protocol is followed for each child's safety and security. Much as attendance for adults can assist in providing congregation care, so also check-ins with children. When parents know their children are cared for and safe, they have even greater respect and appreciation for the congregation.

There are numerous other benefits to a chosen platform, which can be used quite extensively outside of the church as your congregation begins their missional push into the community. I urge you to take the time to consider various platforms, adopt one that works best within the congregation, and can be wisely budgeted for each year.

Communication Capabilities

One of the essential daily benefits of having the information on a connected platform is the availability of immediate and broad communication. When deciding which platform to use for the congregation, consider the ability of that platform to connect to texting services, email, and social media. I have used several platforms for communication through text and email: PastorsLine[33] (text) and Constant Contact[34] (email). Another is Flocknote[35], which gives text, email and limited congregational management. Lastly, I have employed a voice system to send verbal messages each week, and when an urgent message needs to be transmitted to the congregation. OneCall Now[36] has been my go-to resource for this need.

When previous congregations have used Planning Center Online, each external communications platform has been able to sync right to selected groups allowing texts and emails to be as broad as the entire congregation or narrowly focused on a specific group, be it administrative or study group. When names are added to each group or dropped if they move from the

---

[33] https://pastorsline.com
[34] https://www.constantcontact.com
[35] https://flocknote.com
[36] https://www.onsolve.com/platform-products/critical-communications/one-call-now/

congregations, the lists on these services, and others equipped to sync with the chosen platform, will add or delete accordingly.

There is another complete chapter on the need for communication as well as why and what needs to be communicated. If the required tools are not in place, it will make communication much more difficult. Numerous other platforms and apps are coming online each month, so consider what is relevant for the congregation you serve. Slack has recently become a fantastic tool for inter-team communication, project planning and awareness. WhatsApp has jumped in the lead for some congregations for smaller groups texting and connecting. Form a team, if you can, three to four tech-savvy people who are aware of what is available and possible, yet also mindful of each age group that will need to interact with the communication resource. Having the congregation's and new guest's information on these platforms will be effective for future communication.

A Relevant Fundamental

There are numerous benefits to these platforms, too many to address in this chapter. I encourage exploring available options and discovering what would suit your congregation. When used correctly, these tools build quality relationships between leadership and members, member-to-member, and as a congregation focuses outward into the community to welcome new guests. With minimal costs involved implementing a chosen platform, the return on investment is significant in the efficient understanding and management of a congregation.

These tools are helpful for all leaders and will be appreciated by every leader who steps into a new role including future new pastors. I have often looked back at earlier ministry and realized what a deficit it had been not to have accurate and current information on members and guests and the breakdown of relationships that resulted. Having these tools at a pastor's fingertips is an advantage that cannot be under-appreciated. These connected relationships, provided through congregation management on specific platforms, will help your congregation build a strong foundation for future relevancy.

7

INTENTIONAL DISCIPLESHIP

One of the final commands given by Jesus was to make disciples (Mathew 28:19). Yet, for many congregations it remains an afterthought. There is talk about the importance of discipleship, because leaders recognize it is what their congregation should be doing. Still, there is often a failure to be intentional about biblical discipleship. The significant number of people who escape out the "back door" of a congregation indicate that intentional discipleship has not been the priority it should be. The languishing spirituality and lack of spiritual growth of many members within the congregations across North America is the clearest indicator that intentional discipleship has not been a priority.

The Lack of Intentional Discipleship

Barna Research conducted a survey from December 2020 through January 2021, asking Christian adults some key questions on discipleship. The published results[37] are not surprising, sadly. Of those 2,511 polled, **39%** stated they were not engaged in discipleship; while **28%** of respondents said they were involved in discipleship community. The finding which gave me the greatest pause was the **5%** who said they were discipling others. In a parallel question to a reduced number of respondents, they were asked the reasons they were not involved in active discipleship. "I haven't thought about

---

[37] Barna Research, *Two in Five Christians are Not Engaged in Discipleship* (https://www.barna.com/research/christians-discipleship-community/), Accessed June 14, 2022

Intentional Discipleship

it," **36%** said. The second-highest response, at **35%**, was, "I haven't found someone who I would want to have this kind of relationship with." These recent responses tell the church within the United States that discipleship has not been intentional and is severely lacking in most congregations, severely limiting the spiritual growth of members.

The more significant indicator may be how professed believers interact with the world around them and what non-Christians see in their witnesses. Most are left unimpressed by those who claim to be Christ-followers. Dallas Willard succinctly nails the view of those who observe many of today's professed Christians. "But there is a great deal of disappointment expressed today about the character and effects of Christian people, about Christian institution, and—at least by implication—the Christian faith and understanding of reality."[38] I subscribe much of the blame to the church's failure to place intentional discipleship at the forefront. The process of discipleship is necessary to Christianity. Dietrich Bonhoeffer believes so too; "Christianity without the living Christ is inevitably Christianity without discipleship, and Christianity without discipleship is always Christianity without Christ."[39] All three must work together in harmony.

The next fundamental of *Intentional Discipleship* is one that needs no formal introduction but needs to be reintroduced into many congregations today. In many ways, this is the tipping point of a congregation, from just getting by, to fulfilling the Great Commission with effectiveness.

The Congregation and Discipleship

Author and church consultant Aubrey Malphurs firmly states the urgency and position of discipleship within the local congregation. "Jesus was clear about his church. It wasn't just to teach or preach the Word, as important as that is. Nor was it evangelism alone, although this is emphasized as much as teaching. He expected his entire church (not simply a few passionate disciple-makers) to move people along a maturity or disciple-making continuum from pre-birth (unbelief) to the new birth (belief) and then to maturity."[40] Malphurs

---

[38] Dallas Willard, *The Great Commission: Reclaiming Jesus' Essential Teachings on Discipleship* (New York: Harper Collins, 2006), Introduction
[39] Dietrich Bonhoeffer, *The Cost of Discipleship* (New York: Touchstone, 1995), 59
[40] Aubrey Malphurs, *Strategic Disciple Making* (Grand Rapids: Baker Books, 2009), 19

Leading a Congregation to Relevance

rings the bell and makes a clarion call for discipleship to become a priority within congregations. Intentional discipleship should become a top focus within the congregation, from children to mature adults. Clear evidence of successful implementation into the congregation's culture will become apparent in the lives of each member as they interact with one another and unbelievers.

In pastoring for two decades, I admit I failed early at making intentional discipleship a priority. My denominational leaders never actually made it a measure of success with pastors and local congregations. Decisions for Christ and baptisms were a key metric, but never the discipleship process that led to or followed the decision. I knew it was a process each member should engage in. Still, the measurement of discipleship success was not a priority, so intentional discipleship was not a priority for myself or the congregation I pastored. We measure what we treasure. Truth.

One step further, if I may. The importance of doctrines, as held by a denomination, and the decision to believe in God often comes to the forefront when sharing with individuals as we practice public evangelism. Does an individual understand what the Bible says about specific doctrines or beliefs, as held by the denomination (check mark), and will there be a personal decision (check mark) that indicates they understand and will decide to believe in Jesus, and the doctrines? Doctrine and decision, without intentional discipleship is a recipe for failure in a new Christian's start to their spiritual journey. We need more than just doctrines and decisions; we need transformation. Jesus sought the change that came from relationship. So should we.

"Transformation only comes through the discipleship that is centered on Jesus."[41] Without the relationship, there is no individual transformation that requires more than knowing about God but knowing Him personally. Understanding and growing in the beliefs as championed are important as it relates to discipleship but should come from a relationship with God grounded in love.

We do well to consider the first thing Jesus told us to do in the Great Commission: "Go, therefore, and *make disciples* ..." Matthew 28:19 ESV, *emphasis mine*. Following that with baptizing (decision) and teaching (doctrine) to be done afterward. By this order, one could correctly assume

---

[41] Eric Geiger, Michael Kelley, Phillip Nation, *Transformational Discipleship* (Nashville: B&H, 2012), 9

Intentional Discipleship

discipleship is a process of transformation that begins before an individual makes a personal decision to believe in Christ, the pre-requisite to salvation. The journey of discipleship continues after this decision. At the same time, doctrines (beliefs) are being learned and fully understood. There is also a process of personal transformation, one that changes the focus from things in life previously enjoyed to those things that are of God. This takes place as the Holy Spirit leads and convicts. The speed at which an individual progresses on their spiritual journey varies from person to person. It can't be forced by the congregation or individual members. There is no self-selected conduct committee that can determine if a person is growing sufficiently or at the correct pace. It is a God-process, and He leads the way.

If nothing else positive comes from this book and its *Congregation Development Model*, I hope the intense desire to be intentional about discipleship becomes a priority for your congregation and your ministry.

Relevant congregations will make disciples, irrelevant congregations do not. How do we know? Authors Geiger, Kelley, and Nation make this conclusion from their many observations of the church today. "Since Christ-centered discipleship results in transformation, we can confidently assert that most churches are deficient in discipleship … For a church to be deficient in discipleship is to be deficient in its fundamental reason for existence."[42] If your congregation qualifies to be part of the previous statement, it now remains for your congregation to determine whether to no longer be deficient in discipleship practices. Ask instead how that will be accomplished and what implemented objectives would achieve an intentional Christ-centered discipleship culture within your congregation.

The Processes of Discipleship

Discipleship efforts should reach all ages, from children to mature adults and everyone in the middle. Children, youth, and young adult programs should be centered on intentional discipleship and the adult teaching programs a congregation develops for the weekend and any day between regular services. Intentional small groups of varying types, for developing relationships and

---

[42] Geiger, Kelley, Nation.10,11

disciples, are a crucial part of intentionality and a fundamental to be discussed in another chapter.

Two critical areas in adopting a culture of discipleship-making are curriculum and characteristics. What programs and materials will be used to reach people of different spiritual levels, from unbelief to full spiritual maturity? There are significant resources available for congregations to use and systems to be put into place to keep the cycle moving forward.

Partnering personal characteristics to the curriculum is vital because that shows new disciples what a fully committed disciple of Christ looks like. I once attended a seminar by David Beuhring, author of several books on discipleship. He ruminated that many within the church didn't feel qualified to teach or exhibit discipleship because they didn't know enough or act enough like a disciple. His response to those individuals was simple, "All it takes is knowing one more thing, or doing one more thing, than the person you are discipling." Teach through a chosen curriculum, model with character, and begin developing new disciples.

Also, please don't underestimate the power of discipling in a one-to-one style either. There are many who don't grow as well in groups as they do individually. The best place to begin this practice is to model it personally for others within the congregation. Prayerfully ask God to provide the first person of the same gender He would like you to spend the next year discipling. In due course, this will be revealed to you. When the person God has chosen becomes evident, share with them your desire to intentionally disciple another person, asking if they would like to join you in that mentoring relationship for the coming year. Find out where they are in their spiritual journey, and prayerfully walk with them deliberately in the coming months. As you get four months into the process with the individual you're discipling, ask them to now select someone they can in turn replicate the process.

One more thing occurs from a one-on-one process of discipleship. The person who is discipling another feels the urgency to grow deeper roots spiritually themselves and be a person who models the characteristics of a disciple of Jesus.

Intentional Discipleship

The Characteristics of a Disciple

How does a leader know intentional discipleship is working within their congregation? The behaviors of individuals begin to change, transform if you will, reflecting Christ to family, friends, and more importantly, to the world around them. The first indicator comes directly from Jesus, "By this all people will know that you are My disciples: if you have love for one another." John 13:35 *ESV*. When love for one another becomes more apparent within the congregation, it is a reasonably strong indicator that intentional discipleship is bearing fruit. A person comes into church hoping to find something different within the building than they find in the world. Genuine love for one another would undoubtedly qualify as a difference!

Further characteristics of a committed and growing disciple, as I have observed through experience, are:

- *Spends deliberate time with God through Bible study, prayer, and other disciplines.*
- *Makes God the center of their worship experience, personally and corporately.*
- *Treats others with genuine love, compassion, kindness, and forgiveness.*
- *Serves others, without qualification, in humility, giving graciously for another's benefit.*
- *Stewards the resources of time, talent, and treasure given to them by God.*
- *Shares the compelling power of the gospel with others by example and testimony.*
- *Seeks opportunities to intentionally disciple others, whether new or existing.*

There may be many other characteristics you would add to this list. Still, I have seen these seven consistently with those who profess to follow Christ wholeheartedly and exhibit characteristics of a committed disciple. If all who declared they were Christians had these traits in their life, we would never need another evangelistic series or purposeful effort to convince people that God matters. The proof would be in the people, and in today's world these committed disciples would stand out like bold colors in a monotone world of darkness.

Final Thoughts on Discipleship

Intentional, Christ-centered, transformational discipleship matters. Jesus chose twelve men from the many people who followed Him, pouring Himself into them for three-plus years through teaching and example. Except for Judas, the disciples transformed to look more like Jesus and were ultimately used by God to set their first century world on fire with a powerful witness and testimony of the gospel. The process of intentional discipleship takes time, but the value is that as one life changes for the better, others are changed by the result of it.

The spiritual leader must be a committed disciple who models the characteristics of one called by God. The congregation's spirituality will rarely rise above the leader's spirituality. I encourage you to take a personal inventory of your spiritual life and ask yourself if you are a committed disciple who models the characteristics of one. I know this to be true: the congregation most values what the leader values and will reflect their leader. If God is not transforming the heart of the leader, most likely the hearts of the members are not being transformed either, the goal of discipleship. If you emphasize intentional discipleship as a value in your life and leadership, exemplified by teaching and character, your congregation will do so also.

8

DEVELOPING LEADERS AND TEAMS

One of the greatest gifts a leader can share is mentoring another leader. Biblical examples are numerous; Moses and Joshua, Elijah and Elisha, Eli and Samuel, Paul and Timothy, Barnabas and Mark, to name a few. Of course, the most significant example is Jesus, who took twelve apprentices and poured Himself into them, building the early church leaders. When a seasoned leader's knowledge and wealth of experience are given to a new leader, the results can be extraordinary. It requires a humble spiritual leader willing to give of themselves to another, knowing the mentored leader may one day be known as even more significant than the mentor. However, spiritual leaders are called to multiply and invest in others, results notwithstanding.

As a spiritual leader, you are responsible for pouring yourself into another person so God can develop them into a spiritual leader also. It is a daunting task and requires an amount of responsibility and accountability few are willing to undertake. It also could be considered mandatory for spiritual leaders. Aubrey Malphurs and Will Mancini share their perspective. "The job of the leader isn't just to enlist followers but to recruit and equip more and better leaders. It's the leader's responsibility to develop other leaders."[43] Notice the key word they used? Responsibility. Of the many duties you have as a leader, developing leaders cannot be abandoned.

---

[43] Aubrey Malphurs and Will Mancini, *Building Leaders* (Grand Rapids: Baker Books, 2004), 26

What could be the negative within the congregation if you don't intentionally develop other leaders? "Failure to develop emerging leaders puts the future of any ministry in serious jeopardy."[44] Does that seem like hyperbole? I don't think so. The evidence in many congregations shows the truth of this statement. Programs and ministries running on empty due to a lack of developed leaders to keep them operating effectively.

Additionally, wise spiritual leaders understand what Solomon meant when he wrote, "Two are better than one, because they have a good return for their labor." Ecclesiastes 4:9. The best work is done when more than one is involved, which means investing in individuals and teams of individuals. When appropriately exercised, Solomon's other maxim is proved; "A cord of three strands is not quickly broken." (4:12). I encourage every leader to welcome the opportunity of *Developing Leaders & Teams,* which is the next fundamental to consider in the development model. These are both ongoing works of the leader.

The Importance of Development

In the Disney/Pixar movie, *Cars 3*, Lightning McQueen takes on a new and unexpected role as a mentor. In the original movie, *Cars*, McQueen finds himself in need of some mentoring to provide needed growth and perspective, provided by the Fabulous Hudson Hornet. Ending up in Radiator Springs, the fictional town in the desert West, McQueen learns that going it alone is not the recipe for success, and he needs the wiser, experienced viewpoint of Doc Hudson. This mentor/mentee partnership leads to many subsequent wins on the Cup circuit and a new reputation as a proven winner.

In *Cars 3* Lightning is introduced to Cruz Ramirez, who takes on the role of Lightning's trainer when he is injured. Yet, being a trainer is not the goal for Ramirez, she wants to be a race car, experiencing the victories that McQueen and others have, and has not been given the opportunity to do so. Those opportunities have not presented themselves due to stereotypes and biases from the other race cars, and her employer. In time McQueen sees in Ramirez what Doc Hudson saw in him, and he challenges her to pursue her dream of racing. Not only that, but McQueen mentors Ramirez toward that dream, imparting his years of experience into his young protégé

---

[44] *Malphurs and Mancini,* 26

Developing Leaders and Teams

In the closing scene, the defining race that will prove to everyone McQueen is back in true form, McQueen realizes the dream of his success isn't complete unless Cruz Ramirez becomes a winner too. Halfway through the race McQueen takes himself out, being replaced by Ramirez, allowing her to finish, which she does with a win. The theme of *Cars 3*? McQueen mentors Ramirez, giving the best of himself to her success, and he succeeds as well. Everyone on the Rust-Eze team became a winner due to an intentional decision of mentoring the next generation.

Leaders Invest in Leaders

"Great leaders—the truly successful leaders in the top one percent—all have one thing in common. They know that acquiring and keeping good people is a leader's most important task ... People can grow, develop, and become more effective if they have a leader who understands their value."[45] John Maxwell has it right. The best leaders I have met, and those I have read about, invest in others, making the recipients successful leaders. Yet there are many other good leaders I have observed who are protective of their leadership, afraid to share it with others as if they will diminish themselves—quite the opposite is true. Selfish leaders unwilling to pour into others will soon fade from memory.

One mark of a successful leader is the trail of developed leaders who are successful and in turn develop new leaders. College football coach Nick Saban, famous for his leadership of the Crimson Tide (Alabama NCAA football), has a significant "coaching tree" of individuals who were mentored by him and went on to head coach positions with noted successes. As of this writing, there is Jimbo Fisher (Texas A&M), Steve Sarkisian (Texas), Lane Kiffin (Ole' Miss.), Kirby Smart (Georgia), Mark Dantonio (Michigan State), as well as a few others who did not fare so well on their own. Each coach listed has taken their respective programs to a different level and owes much of their success to the mentoring of Coach Saban and the "Saban Way." The reward for one coach, Kirby Smart, Georgia, was to beat his mentor and the Crimson Tide in the 2022 NCAA Championship game, 33-18.

Within the church work, two opposite examples are telling. Dr. Henry

---

[45] John Maxwell, *Developing the Leaders Around You* (Nashville: Thomas Nelson, 1995), 2

Wright, who concluded his pastoral leadership after fifty-five plus years, left a legacy of pastors and congregational leaders whom he mentored and developed into leaders of people. He intentionally mentored pastors who worked on the staff with him as well as leaders within the congregations and organizations he served. He also had the opportunity as a professor to teach hundreds of students who came through the classroom. Wright understood the principle of leadership multiplication and benefits for God's work.

The opposite example is an individual who served in a significant lead role for twenty years within their organization. This leader, of whom I am well-acquainted, micro-managed other subordinate leaders within the organization. While to some observers, it appeared as though this individual was cultivating leaders, they never really poured themselves into another leader effectively, which would have ultimately led towards the mentored leader's success. There was no strong legacy of leadership development, albeit some within the organization did move on to other successful roles elsewhere, many others did not. This leader, of which I share their example, concluded their role as leader of the organization and faded with no measurable legacy in developing future leaders. All that is left is to wonder what might have been if those twenty years of service had been spent intentionally developing leaders. Many potential spiritual leaders were never produced, never able to take their place in a chosen work, all for lack of a leader willing to mentor unselfishly. Organizations starved for great leaders were deprived because a leader who should have developed new leaders did not.

Maxwell sums up these two types of individuals appropriately; "Most leaders have followers around them. They believe the key to leadership is to gain more followers. Few leaders surround themselves with other leaders. The ones who do bring great value to their organization. And not only is their burden lightened, but their vision is carried on and enlarged."[46] The secret to Henry Wright's leadership was gathering and mentoring other leaders. The downfall of the unnamed leader was selfishly hoarding leadership to themself to the detriment of those around them and, ultimately, the organization they led. You will multiply and magnify your leadership by investing in others if you are a spiritual leader. God's most significant leaders always have.

---

[46] Maxwell, 7

Developing Leaders and Teams

A Culture of Leadership Development

A leadership culture is not natural in most organizations and is missing in most congregations today. It must be intentional. In his book, *Leaders Made Here*, Chick-fil-A's Vice President of Leadership, Mark Miller, referred to this. "A leadership culture exists when leaders are routinely and systematically developed, and you have the surplus of leaders ready for the next opportunity or challenge."[47] As a leader, it is your role to foster a culture of development amongst your leaders, beginning first with modeling what spiritual leadership is. The second is finding those within the congregation with potential leadership skills, characteristics, gifts, etc. and then developing them.

Miller's concept of a leadership culture can be defined in five simple steps: 1) *define* leadership, 2) *teach* leadership, 3) *practice* leadership, 4) *measure* leadership, and 5) *model* leadership. These five steps sound easy but will require time and effort to mentor leaders. Most importantly, it requires you as the primary leader to model the desired outcomes. A leadership culture will emerge and become second nature within twelve to eighteen months if purposeful intent is exhibited.

Finding Leaders

The leaders to develop may be sitting around the table at the next board meeting. Some serve in various capacities within the congregation. Others will be hiding in plain sight, sitting in the pews waiting to be asked if they would like to be mentored. Wherever they are, trust God already knows who they are. Why? Because even though you and I lack the personal wisdom and insight to know and decide who exhibits the leadership capacity, God does not. As spiritual leaders who lean on God for wisdom and discernment, we can trust Him to lead us to those ready to be developed and mentored.

One of my favorite stories of the Bible is Samuel sent on an errand by God to anoint the successor to Saul (1 Samuel 16:1-13). Samuel meets the first of Jesse's sons, Eliab, and believes him to be the next king of Israel. God's response? "Do not consider his appearance or his height, for I have rejected

---

[47] Mark Miller, *Leaders Made Here: Building a Leadership Culture* (San Francisco: Berrett-Koehler, 2017), 1

him. The Lord does not look at the things people look at. People look at the outward appearance, but the Lord looks at the heart." (7). Samuel continued his search and met seven of Jesse's sons, all with God's firm "no." It was only after Jesse mentions David, who was so unimportant in the eyes of his father and family that he was out tending the sheep, that David was called in, and God told Samuel, "Rise and anoint him; this is the one." (12).

If we look for potential leaders to develop, we will look for who qualifies in man's eyes, not God's. To find the spiritual leaders to invest in, make it a matter of prayer. Trust that God will lead to those He wants for you and others to intentionally develop into the next spiritual leaders to use in His work. Additionally, with a leadership development culture established, every leader being developed will be seeking the next leader to continue the process.

Consider this: you may be surprised just how many leaders there are within the congregation waiting to be taken to another level. They never experienced someone intentional about doing so, and when they do, look out! God will raise the next generation of leaders through you, and your influence and vision will thrive. I have also found there are individuals within the congregation that are acknowledged as highly qualified leaders within their work organization but have never been asked to bring those gifts to the congregational setting. How many congregations have been ultimately deprived of growth and relevancy by lack of finding and mentoring the next great leaders?

There is much more to learn about finding and developing leaders. You may have questions, as John Maxwell alludes to. "Why should you develop leaders? Why should you dedicate time, energy, and resources to help others rise and lead? Is it worth it? Can it make a difference? Does the return warrant all the effort that's required?"[48] If any of these questions seem relevant to you, I urge you to read Maxwell's, *The Leader's Greatest Return*. Your leadership will be enhanced in many ways, and the reward of investing in others and being intentional with their spiritual leadership growth is of eternal value. Your congregation will thank you; your leadership team will thank you, and God will thank you.

---

[48] John Maxwell, *The Leader's Greatest Return* (U.S.A.: Harper Collins Leadership, 2020), XIII

Developing Leaders and Teams

Developing Amazing Teams

The concept of developing strong teams is as crucial as intentionally developing leaders within your congregation. Just because you have a board meeting each month doesn't indicate it is a highly functioning team. I have personally witnessed a colleague swimming upstream due to an ineffective team. Everyone had their ideas and worked against each other; worst of all, my colleague wasn't sure how to work with the group effectively. Great leaders lead great teams; it's that simple. And do not underestimate the importance of highly effective teams in moving vision, mission, and core strategies forward.

I am reminded of a story regarding a pastor who finally left his congregation of ten years. When he arrived to assume the responsibilities of the congregation, he was appalled at the plain white doors on the front of the building and asked the board if they could be painted red to enhance their beauty and the aesthetics of the building. He undertook the task himself, not finding anyone who agreed with him or would do it. Much to his chagrin, as he was leaving town ten years later with the moving van, driving by the church for the final time, he saw a deacon with a paintbrush and can of white paint slowly erasing the pastor's preferences one stroke at a time. No one on the team ever bought into the pastor's vision, primarily because it wasn't a shared vision.

The real lesson in this story is that a leader doesn't move forward without the team coming with them. As a leader, don't dictate, influence. Spiritual leaders influence people to join God's agenda. They don't force issues, demand their way, or do things without getting buy-in and complete ownership in the outcomes. A pastor will come and go, but leaders within the congregation will often be there long after the pastor is gone. As a mentor drilled into my head, "You will go, they will stay. Make sure the church owns it before you move forward with it."

Leading teams is leading unselfishly. Wayne Cordeiro, the lead pastor of New Hope in Hawai'i (someone must do it), authored a poignant statement. "Building teams does not begin with a certain kind of technique, it begins with a certain kind of heart—an unselfish, authentic heart—desiring only God's best. Such a heart constantly asks, "How can I include others?" It anticipates the joy of sharing experiences, struggles, and victories, realizing that, like the body, we work best in teams--the way God designed us to function."[49] Relevant

---

[49] Wayne Cordeiro, *Doing Church as a Team: The Miracle of Teamwork and How it Transforms Churches* (Minneapolis: Bethany House, 2004), 174

congregations are most effective because they work together as a large team (the whole), and small teams (specific ministries, roles, or responsibilities). A leader that develops effective teams will move a congregation further than a leader who does not.

I won't admit it is easy to work with teams. It requires patience, love and a dose of humor. It took a year to decide on a critical component of a church planting venture in one congregation. One year! One decision, but it required the team to work through numerous meetings to get the decision they ultimately agreed upon unanimously. I could have forced it, but they would never have bought into why the decision was necessary. In every meeting, and there were quite a number, I continued to share the ultimate vision of the project, the mission and purpose, as well as the decisions that would affect the outcome. By the time the crucial decision was made, all the individuals were aligned in the same direction to support the decision and, ultimately, the church planting project. I knew one year previous what we should do, but the one year of debate led to the entire team buying into that preferred choice.

We > I

It may appear a little like self-preservation, but as a leader, it's much easier to defend a decision when you can honestly say, "We made the decision," compared to "I made the decision." Of course, the rule of credit still applies. If the decision turned out to be poor, take the blame. Give the team credit if the decision was good, with excellent results. As Lee Iacocca reminds us, "Here's the thing I learned as a CEO. You succeed or fail based on your team."[50] The congregation is much more likely to accept the decision when they know it was done from team consensus, aligning with the agreed-upon strategic vision, mission, and values adopted by the congregation. The best part is this; you may leave, but you won't be watching someone paint the doors back to their original color when you arrived!

I have brought two assessments into the process to strengthen teams in the past. One is a *DISC* assessment, the other *Strengthfinders 2.0* by Clifton. There are others, but I found these two to be the most practical and insightful.

---

[50] Lee Iacocca, with Catherine Whitney, *Where Have All the Leaders Gone?* (New York: Scribner, 2007), 16

Developing Leaders and Teams

I have each team member take them, whether on the leadership team or other teams within the church. A leader learns how to communicate with *DISC* and appreciate the strengths another individual brings by talent and perspective with *Strengthfinders 2.0*. These assessments strengthen the "we" of teams. Patrick Lencioni and The Table Group developed another newer assessment, *The Working Genius*. This quick assessment is a valuable tool in affirming that the right people are in the right place, serving to their potential. There is always a cost involved in these assessments, but I suggest the higher price is the ineffectiveness of a team that has not gone through them.

Achieving it Together

Developed leaders and strong teams bring the best results for more robust vision and mission support, understanding, and communication. There is no better fundamental than developing spiritual leaders and high-functioning spiritual teams to work together toward a common purpose, ultimately bringing your congregation to relevance.

9

THE NEXT GENERATION

"You are here for such a short time. But when you grow up and think back on your childhood, we hope some of your earliest memories are about us, your church ... We are the church, and you child, are precious to us ... Have we loved and entertained you, or have we also created disciples?

With your adult future in mind, are we intentionally raising you to become Christ-following men and women with both spine and heart—spine to stand firm for your Christian beliefs in an increasingly hostile secular world and heart to embrace that same intolerant-of-faith world, with a love that can't be ignored ...

May you know we never stopped loving you. And may that love root you firmly and prepare you for the decades to come when you are the church."[51]

From, *A Letter to Today's Children*

God and Children

O, to have been a child and experienced Jesus from a youngster's viewpoint. While adults in the room acted like adults, with disagreements, doubts, questions, and lack of trust, children saw in Jesus One who exhibited kindness and compassion and, I have no doubt, fun. His presence drew them,

---

[51] Valerie Bell, Christian Marchand, Matt Markins, Mike Handler, *Resilient* (Marceline: Walsworth, 2020), 4-5

The Next Generation

and some of Christ's most touching miracles were to children and youth. When the adults couldn't figure out Jesus, and the disciples tried to keep the children away, Jesus welcomed them. Consider Mark 10:13-16:

"And they were bringing children to Him so that He would touch them; but the disciples rebuked them. But when Jesus saw this, He was indignant and said to them, "Allow the children to come to Me; do not forbid them, for the kingdom of God belongs to such as these. Truly I say to you, whoever does not receive the kingdom of God like a child will not enter it at all." And He took them in His arms and began blessing them, laying His hands on them."

Jesus was a magnet for children. "Wherever the Savior went the benignity of his countenance, and his gentle, kindly manner won the love and confidence of children."[52] But perhaps even more significant was the ministry impact He knew could be made with children, which we as congregational leaders would be wise to consider. Children are open to new ideas and are sponges for information. Simple faith and trust allow children to be reached as no adults can. A small tree can be planted and trained in a specific direction, which ultimately strengthens as it grows, so with children who eventually become mature adults.

I recognize that the fundamental of *The Next Generation* is not always easy to implement. Many congregations are not equipped for under-twenty-one ministry or have lost sight of the urgent need for a relevant ministry program for children, youth, and young adults. When I say relevant, I mean that in the most specific way. I have walked into classrooms that use lessons from decades ago and shy away from helping the next generation meet life where it is today. We use the Bible as our source for teaching but must integrate it into life as it is known today and everything that comes within it. This is intentional discipleship of children, preparing them for adult life with God.

God Loves Children. Do We?

One of the best books on children and youth ministry, and the importance of programs that minister to the next generation, is *Transforming Children into Spiritual Champions,* by George Barna. Written in 2003 and often overlooked,

---

[52] E.G. White, *The Desire of Ages* (Berrien Springs: Types and Symbols, 2019), 602

it is still relevant today and enforces the need for effective ministry to young people. Barna explains why: "Children matter to God because He loves them and wants them to experience the best, right from the start of their lives. He relies upon us, their teachers and protectors, to deliver the guidance and experiences they need to grow in their understanding of love for and obedience to Him."[53] As leaders, we are confident that God loves children. The question then remains, do we and our congregations love them too?

Of course, we love the next generation of kids, youth, and adults, right? But actions speak louder than words. Consider these findings in Barna's then research, "...Signs indicate that children are not a high ministry priority. Among these are the fact that most church leaders we interviewed—pastors, staff, and elders—are uninformed as to the spiritual content and practices related to their children's ministry, and almost none of those church leaders can provide specific insights into how satisfactorily the children are maturing in their faith."[54] This was written in 2003!

By experience, I would say not much has changed in many congregations since Barna initially provided these research findings in his book. Children can be told they are loved, but does the investment of time, money, and measurement by a leader and the congregation prove it?

As a parent and pastor, I have witnessed congregations that say much about caring for the spirituality of the next generation, but the actions say otherwise—rooms with faded paint, stained and ripped carpet, poor lighting, and decades-old musty smells. In some cases, children and youth were shuffled to the last rooms the adults wanted and even then, displaced if the need for adult ministry became more pressing. Just as the overall aesthetic of the facility leads to a great first impression, so do the rooms and area of the building set apart for next-generation ministries. From the children to parents, both will have a clear idea of just how important the children are based on the facility's conditions.

The outdated curriculum has been another issue. I understand we are teaching from the Bible, the foundation for every discipleship course. But when materials look as if they came over on the Titanic, (and I use that purposefully, for I've seen some look as if they were recovered from the

---

[53] George Barna, *Transforming Children into Spiritual Champions* (Ventura: Regal Books, 2003), 46
[54] Barna, 39

The Next Generation

bottom of the ocean!) it's time to reconsider the priority the next generation has within the congregation.

In 2022 I still observe some teachers reading from a script, using flannel boards, and putting their children to sleep in class. We encourage teachers within our schools to update their methodologies and tools of education to reflect new resources and the realities of this generation; why do we not ask the same of our teachers on weekends within our congregations? We can also provide the tools and technology for teachers responsible for the children within the congregation, can't we?

Furthermore, the curriculum used currently may be biblically based but does it help the next generation deal with life? They are dealing daily with issues most adults have not contended with. The walk of discipleship and living in the real world must be part of the teaching and presentations, allowing all ages of young people to understand how God fits in their lives with relevance.

The Updated Facts & Figures

In 2022 Barna Research released their findings from extensive research conducted in 2021.[55] In their study, **54%** of the current next-generation program leaders felt the ministry had been forgotten. Of those same individuals polled, **87%** believed their work within these programs made a long-term difference for young people. Even more urgent is the realization that **92%** of the parents surveyed said the children's ministry was as important as the worship service they attended. The same **92%** affirmed that a quality children's ministry significantly impacted the church they would attend. These are numbers to pay attention to on multiple levels; to encourage increased support for next-generation ministries, support the leaders, and recognize that a quality program promotes growth and relevancy among adults who choose the congregation due to next-generation ministry for their children.

A separate poll conducted in early 2021 gives insight into how parents view their children's spiritual growth and experience and their importance as parents. Among Christians and non-Christians, **73%** of U.S. parents responded that they are concerned about their child's faith development. Of those

---

[55] Barna Research Group, https://www.barna.com/research/childrens-ministry/, Accessed May 31, 2022

respondents who consider themselves Christians, **51%** said they were "very concerned," out of the **80%** who responded affirmatively. Asked if they were concerned about their children staying true to their faith, **58%** of those same Christian parents replied, "very concerned." With increased secularization in first-world countries, and an ever-declining biblical worldview within the church, it's not hard to understand why parents have become concerned about their children's current and future spiritual state. When parents know the congregation, they currently attend, or are about to choose, places an equal or higher value on their children's faith than they do, they will call it home, even if the adult programs are unsatisfactory.

Current Realities for the Next Generation

It may be a tired statement, but that makes it no less accurate: This generation faces challenges and realities my generation didn't meet. There may have been similarities, but with 24/7/365 access to everything in the palms of their hands, the pressure is much greater. I have both a collegiate and high school student in my house. Parenting the youngest, being a girl, I have learned how much stress a young woman is under today to always look her best, keep up with peer pressures, and live up to standards imposed by others. Instagram, TikTok, Snapchat, YouTube, and other platforms are always on. If a young person doesn't fit in, look just right, or adhere to social norms, the comments are filled with ridicule, hate, and behaviors easily classified as bullying.

These online pressures are another layer added to the awkward social growth a young person must undergo in the real physical world. Navigating school from elementary to college is not easy. The "cool" kids can still bully those they don't perceive like themselves. The suicide rate of young people is skyrocketing, with news stories of suicide commonplace among children not even in their teen years as they are bullied and ridiculed to the edge. I cannot even fathom what young people are going through today contrasted to when I grew up in the 70s and 80s. Yet as a pastor and parent, I have become painfully aware of these realities to a level I never expected. Our children need to feel safe in their skin, and the environments most are in leave them with the impression they are not adequate and not wanted. May the congregation you lead provide them a safe place they need and desire, allowing them to feel loved and accepted.

The Next Generation

Throw into the mix injustice, loneliness, identity questions, school shootings, and upticks in crime involving under-eighteen children. With information bombarding them from all directions and their peers, our children are faced with more questions by the age of twenty-one than most adults will in their lifetime. We cannot assume their lives are like ours or that they solve problems as we do. We could not even begin to fully grasp what a young person navigates daily unless we are a parent of one or actively involved in ministry to them in our congregations.

Let's add one more layer to this. If these issues were not enough, there now enters the matter of faith for a young person. They question if there is a Truth. Are there not multiple ways to reach the destination of heaven? Why should they believe an adult when teaching or preaching a biblical certainty? Compounding these issues (and even more not discussed here) is the reality that many of the next generations within our congregations have never been mentored in an active discipleship walk with God. Safe places for doubts and questions are rarely provided within the church walls, so they go outside instead, losing their faith in the process. Kids today believe anything goes and almost everything is acceptable. While we are to accept all humanity, not everything humans do is pleasing to God.

There is much more to be said on this subject, and I would highly recommend you, as a congregation leader, work with your board or leadership team to study in-depth about the next generation and the challenges they are going through. It may be more imperative than ever to better understand how to enable an increasingly effective ministry for all ages of the next generation God has given us the responsibility to raise. The urgency of this fundamental is summed up here: "We strongly believe child discipleship is the most crucial conversation impacting the future of faith."[56] If the next generation has not become the most important conversation in your congregation, it should be.

Prioritizing the Next Generation

Hopefully, there has awakened a more profound desire to minister to the next generation within you and to put forth an honest assessment of the current state of ministry for 0-18 and collegiate level within your congregation.

---

[56] Valerie Bell, Christian Marchand, Matt Markins, Mike Handler, *Resilient* (Marceline: Walsworth, 2020), 17

Walk the halls and classrooms with new eyes. See what the young people see and what parents see when they deliver their children to the trust and care of the leaders. Look over the curriculum and resources used, and the tools provided to teachers so they may teach and minister to their students.

If you want to know what is perceived regarding the ministry for children and youth, put together a survey or hire a third party to come in and assist you. Carefully crafted questions for parents and young people will give you the answers you want, or maybe you are afraid to hear. But we measure what we treasure. I suspect if every congregation is honest with themselves while creating their strategic vision, they will include an initiative for the next generation, one with specific objectives and measurements of success. These should not be limited to how many are in the classroom each week but deeper: measuring spiritual growth, faith, openness, and safe places within the congregation for discussions on their faith, denomination, and more. These are valuable measurements of effectiveness in ministering to young people.

It is urgent to find volunteers who understand young people and minister to them in today's environment, not the one from a decade ago. Each teacher should have a commitment to young people and be willing to train for their position. I have noted some congregations where those teaching were selected because no one else would do it. The teachers were not prepared and ineffective, and the young people in their classes were not engaged.

One last thing regarding volunteers, EVERY person even remotely involved in ministry to the next generation should have a background check. No exceptions. Put a rule in place and a process, that stipulates, "Before any involvement within children, youth, or young adult ministries, a person must have attended within the congregation for six months, have references for previous work in the area of ministry, and undergo a background check." I have heard many stories and experienced firsthand what happens when the wrong person gets around children. Your young people deserve the protection, and parents want the protection. When parents allow their children to enter these spaces within congregations, they want to know their kids are safe.

Moving into the 21st Century

After significant evaluation, curriculum updates will most likely be needed in many congregations today. Your denomination may have specific resources

The Next Generation

or new ones that no one has requested yet. Ask for them and try them out. *Orange*[57] and *Grow*[58] are two separate companies that provide resources across denominations. Having seen both in practice, I can easily recommend each (without financial gain for my endorsement). Both focus on discipleship and the practical application of biblical truths. Both acknowledge that elementary school children are not taught the same as high school children and adjust curriculum accordingly. Both create engagement with parents outside the classroom setting, inviting study and conversation between parents and children throughout the week. Whatever curriculum is used, it should be relevant to the decade we live in, help children navigate the issues in their lives, promote discipleship and personal growth, and reflect God as the Source of life, salvation, and eternal life.

I rarely recommend a "must-read" book, although perhaps some of my former members would disagree. In this case, there is one that should be non-negotiable from congregation leaders to next-generation leaders. *It's Just a Phase, So Don't Miss It*, by Kristen Ivy and Reggie Joiner, is easy to read and one of the best tools for every leader and teacher to understand how to teach to phases of life. Multiple other resources are also available on the website[59], and I recommend them wholeheartedly.

Lastly, update the aesthetics in each area according to age group. A designer in your congregation may be equipped to help with decisions on colors and graphics, or it may be worth hiring someone with the experience. Find out what the different age levels of kids like and find a way to incorporate those preferences. It doesn't have to be so cool that it needs to be repainted in a year or becomes a bad cliché, but it should reflect what the next generation appreciates. Update the tools used by teachers. Install projectors or large screen flat panels, ready to plug a laptop, tablet, or phone into, and that can access Wi-Fi with a safely guarded password. I know this to be true; when the aesthetics are updated and modern, the children and parents recognize this as a concerted effort on the part of the congregation leadership to grow the next generation ministry, and they appreciate the importance of ministering to young people.

---

[57] https://thinkorange.com
[58] https://growcurriculum.org
[59] https://justaphase.com

Engaging the Next Generation

Not all of ministry within the context of the next generation is teaching and activity, it is also mentoring and empowering. As authors Powell, Mulder and Griffin write in their book, *Growing Young*, there is a need to "hand the keys" of leadership over to the next generation.[60] Leaders exhibit "keychain leadership," and are "Intentional about entrusting and empowering all generations, including teenagers and emerging adults, with their own set of keys."[61] Leadership trusts them to take on leadership roles within the congregation at the appropriate time, and involve them in the life of the body, just as we would with adults. This is a valuable part of ministering to the next generation, and one which may have a more significant impact in their long-term spiritual journey than you might think.

When I was ten years old our family moved from the city we lived in to a new home further out in the country. With that move came finding a new church home, which we did, meaning a loss of all current familiarity and friends for me. After a couple weeks in this new church, which was small and only had a couple other kids my age, I felt quite alone and upset. I didn't go unnoticed, however, as Ken, a twentysomething adult, came to me one weekend and asked if I would like to learn how to operate the sound system for the church. With that began a newfound enthusiasm for church attendance, as I was involved in the sound and other elements of service and being active in the church.

The result of that invitation by Ken kept me engaged every week. He did it for other young people too, and we all were better for it. Forty plus years later I am still engaged in church work, but something more beneficial came as a result; I kept connected with God, even when tempted to walk away. Because I appreciated Ken asking me to do simple things that involved activity, I also learned to trust him and listen in spiritual matters. Without he or I really knowing it at the time, he was engaging in intentional discipleship. It paid off. Additionally, forty-five years later Ken and I are still good friends, with both of us active in our journey with God and others.

---

[60] Kara Powell Jake Mulder, and Brad Griffin, *Growing Young* (Grand Rapids: Baker Books, 2016) Ch. 2
[61] *Powell, Mulder, Griffin*, 53

The Next Generation

Be deliberate about engaging the next generation in the life of the congregation. Don't underestimate what it means for them, their parents, and the congregation. It places another aspect of value on young people and contributes to the intentional discipleship culture of the church, just in a different form and process. It is an opportunity not to be missed, with the added benefit of the congregation intentionally "growing young", as Powell, Moulder, and Griffin urge congregations to do by effectively engaging and empowering the next generation.

Why?

The calling of each congregation is to minister to every generation. The younger generation will soon become the next leadership generation. What will their journey of faith look like as they mature? The statistics bear the importance of influencing children for God at a young age. Not indoctrinating, mind you, but teaching them the principles of faith and discipleship. Using the biblical stories to demonstrate to young people that although the characters referred to were not under the relentless pressure of the social media spotlight, they had their challenges. They failed, were forgiven and were loved by God unconditionally. In each story told throughout the Old Testament and New, there is an opportunity to help young people see that faith is practical, God is ever-present, and there are no surprises in life God is not present to help them through.

Most importantly, they must know they are loved unconditionally through everything in their life, by God and the congregation they call home. Living faith is practical faith and is prone to mistakes and failures. We have an opportunity to mentor and disciple the next generation with the same intentionality and passion as we do the adults.

May you have a renewed urgency for the young people in your congregation. May your leadership team have the same commitment, too. Then act on it. Be honest with the realities of the program as it currently exists and take on the challenge to improve it. When parents recognize the congregation's value of their children's current and future spiritual journey, it will positively impact them. Much time and effort are spent evangelizing and being missional in the community, working diligently for individuals we have not yet met, while overlooking the harvest God has brought into the congregation through young people. Like Jesus, may we welcome the next generation of disciples with open hearts filled with genuine love and acceptance.

This may be the most important chapter regarding the future of the church. It is the one which could most likely impact the future relevance of a congregation. Each child and young adult are a gift, may our congregations value them as God does.

10

COMMUNICATING FOR RESULTS

"Finding a good message and then sticking with it takes extraordinary discipline, but it pays off tenfold in the end ... The overwhelming majority of your customers or constituents aren't paying as much attention as you are."[62] And with that, Frank Luntz identifies our frustrations with communicating to the congregation and community-at-large. We think if it was told to them a couple of times, they heard it. Yet how often as a leader has a member or attendee said they were not aware an event was taking place, or a team meeting scheduled? You insist it was communicated promptly and efficiently, and you just can't explain why the information transmitted gets so few results.

Even worse, as a leader, there is a consistent need to be communicating the vision to the congregation, and many times there will be those who never seem to have heard it. It can be tempting to blame those who haven't heard what we think has been communicated quite often, but Andy Stanley suggests the blame lies elsewhere. "We are tempted at times to blame the people around us for their inability to understand and act on the vision we have cast. If the followers don't get it, we probably haven't delivered the vision in a way that makes it get-able."[63] In other words, the leader didn't communicate it as well as they thought they had; thus, people never heard it. In that case, the onus is on the leader to learn how to better communicate with effectiveness.

---

[62] Frank Luntz, *Words that Work* (New York: Hachette, 2008), 12
[63] Andy Stanley, *Making Vision Stick* (Grand Rapids: Zondervan, 2007), 17

Leading a Congregation to Relevance

Why are the communicated messages not getting through? Here are some considerations: "It has been suggested that the average consumer is exposed to up to *10,000 brand messages a day* ... The average attention span of a customer has dropped to just *8 seconds*, which is lower than the 9-second attention span of a goldfish ... Consumers are likely to switch between screens up to 21 times an hour."[64] (italics mine.) Small wonder communication, which we believe to be adequate, is not achieving the intended results. "Remember, you may be making yourself sick by saying the exact same thing for the umpteenth time, but many in your audience will be hearing it for the very first time."[65] The following fundamental to discover and understand is the right communication which makes a difference. "Clarity is the preoccupation of the effective leader. If you do nothing else as a leader, be clear."[66] Therefore, *Intentional Communication* is a vital fundamental for every leader and congregation.

The Need for Relevant Communication

In his 2019 book release, *Rethink Communication*, Phil Bowdle points out how the church communicates today is much different from what it was doing was several decades ago. The problem is that many churches are still using communication styles from those previous decades. What is the primary difference today? "Thirty years ago, the church's greatest communication opportunities were inside the walls of the church. Today, the greatest communication opportunities are outside the church."[67] Think about this: the church communicated to members and attendees who ventured into the church for decades. They were presented with a bulletin that shared events and updates and would receive further communication within the services. Some churches did send out newsletters, but even that was "old news" when it arrived. If it was urgent, a phone chain was in place to communicate the timely information, usually centered around a crisis.

---

[64] Eventeem, *"The Attention Economy and your Business' 'Scarcest Resource in 2019"* (https://eventeem.co.uk/attention-economy-2019/), Accessed May 11, 2022

[65] Frank Luntz, *Words that Work* (New York: Hachette), 12

[66] Marcus Buckingham, as quote by Will Mancini, *Church Unique* (San Francisco: Jossey-Bass, 2008), 51

[67] Phil Bowdle, *Rethink Communication: A Playbook to Clarify and Communicate Everything in Your Church* (Los Angeles: Center for Church Communication, 2019), 36

Communicating for Results

Today, as Bowdle writes, the digital platform has changed how we communicate within our congregation and our community. There is still the service and bulletin to consider but add to that social media (Facebook, Instagram, Snapchat, TikTok, etc.), Web, Email, Video (YouTube, Vimeo, Facebook Live, etc.), text, and phone calls. As daunting as this appears to those trained in communicating through the earlier methods of in-person, bulletin, and newsletter, the changes in communication routes are exciting and open a new world of opportunity to share the gospel.

Changing How the Congregation Communicates

For many churches, this seems a near-impossible task. Here is why, Bowdle writes: "Communication in the church is no longer an administrative task. It's not confined to managing a weekly bulletin. Delivering your message effectively requires tapping into creative skills like writing, editing, video, photography, graphic design, and storytelling to creatively tells tell the story of what God is doing in and through your church.[68] As a pastor or congregational leader, you don't have the bandwidth to undertake what is needed to communicate to this depth of need. However, within most congregations, there do exist individuals who have that bandwidth; ones who engage in this method of communication every week. These youth and young adults would often welcome an opportunity to serve in the capacity of digital communication, using techniques they are fluid with to serve God in a needed ministry. I'd encourage you to use them!

Larger churches may be available to hire a Minister of Communication, a person trained and equipped to navigate most of the digital methods, equipped with creative writing skills, photography, graphic design, and a passion for communicating the gospel. Yes, it costs money to hire such a person. But, as in many things, consider what it may cost if you don't. The opportunities that exist within the community around your church are endless. The church that understands the power of communication and how it can be effectively used as a 21st Century evangelism and discipleship tool will increase in relevant.

For small congregations, perhaps there is another option. Create a network with other smaller churches within your denomination and within proximity to

---

[68] Bowdle, 39

your congregation's location, if possible, defined by judicatory or conference boundaries. Come together and hire a communications director to help each church learn how to effectively message and create messaging for the different congregations if needed. This communications director could recruit volunteers within each congregation they'll work with, training them in the effective use of platforms, creative writing, design, photography, videography, and more. Each church shares the cost of hiring this communications director, perhaps adjusted by membership and attendance. For those who object due to cost, I repeat that the cost of not doing so may be higher.

Principles of Effective Communication

There are some timeless principles of communication, many strengthened through trial and error. Even with digital platforms, the methods are relevant to effective communication. What are these basic principles? Credible, creative, concise, clear, and consistent messaging. There are others, for sure, but these are the ones I have found time and again to be the most useful while communicating to the congregation and community. If they are implemented through your messaging, be it a weekly sermon, casting vision, or sharing announcements, the results will be noticed within a short time frame regardless of the platform.

Credible: Is your congregation trusted? Are you? Are the words you speak and communicate accurately and quickly backed up by fact? A sermon can be fact-checked while the listener is in the pew, watching from the sofa, or attending via the metaverse. When I see or hear a person or message misrepresents a fact or blatantly ignore it, I question credibility in other areas. *Falsus in uno, falsus in omnibus.* Meaning, false in one thing, false in all things. Don't repost items unless they are credible, and the source can be verified. Once an individual questions credibility, any further efforts will be in vain.

Creative: There are multiple ways to communicate a message. If a picture is worth a thousand words, use powerful images to assist in presenting a point. If sharing an event or invite, what ways would get someone's attention rather than a 10pt font? Use vibrant color and graphics that invite a person to give their eight seconds of attention to your message. Use a short video produced with good lighting and framing techniques to provide a vision recast, quick devotional, invite to an event, or remind of an important date on the calendar. Don't be stale, be unique!

Communicating for Results

Concise: If eight seconds of attention is all you can expect, then each message sent must capture it with straightforward language. If communicating an event, include the event name, date, time, and location (obviously with creativity). Devotional? Great thoughts can be expressed in less than 60 seconds (with a linked invite to learn more). When writing an email message, do so and then return in an hour and rewrite it for conciseness. Consider bullets of information in the opening of the email with details further down in the body. Whichever digital platform you use, be concise with easily located invites embedded for people to get more info.

Clear: Some may argue this is the same as concise, but how often have you read or heard a concise message that isn't clear. What do you want a person to take from the message you preach each week? What is the desired action from the individual? In general, what responses are you seeking from communication? Attend an event? Give to a cause? Rally around the vision? The message should be clear about what the intended call to action is. Words without correct punctuation can make a message quite unclear. In concise messages or lengthy emails, the proper punctuation assists with a clear message. Being clear is crucial for a leader.

Consistent: Remember Frank Luntz's quote at the opening of the chapter? This is consistent communication. Every platform used should have the same message. What they find in the bulletin, online, on Facebook, email, etc., should be consistent with the others. Every statement leading up to an event or action should reflect the same consistency. When casting vision, consistency is the priority. With so much competing for an audience's attention, a consistent message is key to getting an individual to notice and respond.

Final Random Thoughts

A few things bother me about communication that is repeated by many congregations. I am using the close of the chapter to communicate them to you.

Website: Please make it attractive. Update information as needed. Not many care about what happened six months ago. Mobile friendly is essential. The website is the front door to the church. Does it invite? Have location and service times easy to access? Consider a page designed just for guests, easily accessed with a visible link on the main page.

Signs: Fix the lights, reattach the letters, whatever needs to be done for it to present well. If using a sign with plastic letters, please change it out often, and if a letter falls off, find it and put it back. Consider investing in a large LED sign (remember, what you see standing 20 feet away isn't the same as driving by.) No one ever regretted getting a larger sign at purchase. When you do get the new sign, don't use small fonts on the display; be concise and creative to capture people's attention.

Banners: If you must put a banner up to make an announcement, or invite the public to an event, do it right! Bold and creative. Fonts LARGE and quickly read from across the street—event name, date, time. People can't read banners with small fonts and the length of an essay. Concise, clear, and creative! Don't forget to take it down when the event is over.

Digital Displays: Are you sharing information on displays within the building, especially the sanctuary? Concise, clear, and creative are still the best rules. I've seen lots of information on one slide. People can't read it; they ignore it. Break it up into multiple slides if the information is essential. Make it beautiful. Use nature pictures and unique backgrounds. If using a photo with an announcement, the image should enhance the announcement, helping to embed it into the observer's mind. Watch font colors on backgrounds, so they stand out, not washed out.

Pastor's PowerPoints: I use Keynote because I like Apple. If you don't like Apple, you should, and you too can use Keynote. Either way, please don't put your whole sermon outline on one slide or bullet points on a slide and then read them off while preaching. Visuals matter, and people remember what they see (80% recall) more often than what they hear (10%)[69]. Visuals with your sermons can have as much, or more, staying power than what you preach verbally. Make beautiful slides. Be concise and clear. They are an addition to your sermon, not the sermon itself. If you don't know how to do this, find a creative person in your church who can. Take a class. Use semi-prepared slides.[70] Just stop the ugly. Your audience will thank you, especially the younger ones.

Posters and Signs: When the advertised event is over, please take it down. Thank you.

---

[69] iDashboards, UK. (https://medium.com/@iDashboards_UK/on-average-people-remember-only-20-of-what-they-read-but-80-of-what-they-see-8411224769e2.0, Accessed June 3, 2022

[70] www.ignittemedia.com is my favorite source for announcement and sermon slides.

Last Word

If it got lost in everything else in the chapter, remember one thing. "Clarity is the preoccupation of the effective leader. If you do nothing else as a leader, be clear." Hopefully, that was clear, concise, consistent, if not quite creative. You have a message, as does your congregation, about vision, strategy, sermon, announcements, and everything in between. Now is the time to learn how to communicate effectively. If you are not sure how to do so personally, take some courses on effective communication, whether written, spoken, or through platforms. I have listened to men and women whom I respect, who have a superb message, which gets lost in delivery. The same goes for the vision and other crucial parts of their ministry that they are trying to communicate. The message, ineffectively delivered, gets muddied and lost in translation to the listener.

Do not underestimate what intentional communication skills can do for your ministry, and for the congregation as they move forward with purpose and missional outreach. God has given you much to say; learn how to communicate it well and see the difference it will make.

11

ENGAGING THE BODY

Some time ago, I attended a church with a very creative children's story presented by middle-school children to the younger ones in the congregation. Each presenting child represented a different part of the human body. One of them, the "mouth," determined it was the most critical part of the body and declared it so to the rest of the body, leading to an "uprising" of the other body parts represented. The brain stated the mouth would have nothing to say if not instructed to do so. The eyes told the mouth it would have nothing to talk about if there was nothing to see. Each part became upset at being minimized, leading to disunity and a fracturing of the body.

Fortunately for the small children watching, the "body" got itself together and began to realize that no matter the part, its use, or how big or small each one was, all served an essential function. They accomplished more than the individual parts ever could. While the children's story had a successful conclusion with the body working together in harmony, many a congregation is still trying to figure out how best to use their individual parts to accomplish God's mission and become relevant.

The Fully Functional Congregation

A relevant, fully functioning congregation knows how to work together effectively, and each member and regular attendee is engaged in the mission. The *Gifts and Engagement* fundamental helps a congregation achieve this

Engaging the Body

goal. As discipleship introduces the importance of service, a leader helps individuals discover their gifts and how to best use them. This continues the culture of developing disciples who live out service in the context of the local congregation. The organization is static, the congregation is dynamic. Jesus didn't become head of an organization with great structure, but the head of a living organism, the body, with fully functioning parts which require unity to work effectively. A body of believers is active in service and mission.

"Living organisms are, in many aspects, quite similar to organizations, while in other ways they are very different. Both require structure, direction, measurable objectives and leadership. On the other hand, an organism is a living entity with emotions, changes, natural growth and a susceptibility to disease, accidents, predators and sickness. The church, or the Body of Christ, is a living organism."[71] Like a physical body, when one part is in pain, other parts also suffer. When one becomes physically deformed, the other parts compensate for it. The physical body is a living organism, and it must be active to survive and thrive.

I went through a triple-bypass procedure a year before writing this book. The recovery time was two months, but I was determined to jump-start and overachieve. Within several days of being home, I walked different periods of the day, and within two weeks was up to two miles a day and more. What slowed my progress was a simple issue, or so I thought. Without knowing it, I previously fractured my two inner toes on the right foot, and they healed incorrectly. With the additional walking I was doing, the body tried to compensate for this incorrect healing and transferred the weight to the outside of my foot. Within a few weeks, I had a whole other issue to deal with--one so severe I was days from an amputation of my right foot. Having to be off my feet changed my healing dynamic. I gained weight, lost the lung capacity I had been accumulating, and several other minor issues cropped up.

Every part of the physical body, a living organism, has a vital role in a human's overall health and viability. And, just as every part of the human body is essential, so it is within the living organism of the *ekklēsia*, the Body of Christ, of which He is the Head.

---

[71] Wayne Cordeiro, *Doing Church as a Team* (Minneapolis: Bethany House, 2004), 175

The Ekklēsia of Jesus

Standing in Caesarea-Phillipi several years ago, looking up to the granite-faced mountain, I listened to Richard Davidson, Professor of Old Testament Studies at Andrews University, reflect on the interaction between Jesus and Peter. Found in Matthew 16:13-20, Jesus was asking the disciples who people said He was. "Elijah, John the Baptist, a prophet," they responded. Then Jesus asked them directly, "But who do you yourselves say that I am?" (15), upon which Peter immediately replied, "You are the Christ, the Son of the living God." (16). At this point, the promise of the church was launched, but not as we think of church today. "And I also say to you that you are Peter, and upon this rock I will build My church; and the gates of Hades will not overpower it." (18). Much has been written in commentaries on the word "church" as Christ used it, but it is much more straightforward than many make it to be. Leaving the other parts of the text for another discussion, let's focus on one word: church.

In the Greek, what has been translated as "church" is the word, *ekklēsia*. For those who like phonetics, it is pronounced Ek-klay-see'-ah. The Strong's number is G1577 and is defined as "a calling out that is (concretely) a popular meeting especially a religious congregation (Jewish synagogue or Christian community of members on earth or saints in heaven or both): - *assembly* church." *(Italics mine.)* To look further into *ekklēsia*, we turn to Thayer's, which defines the word as, "a gathering of citizens called out from their homes into some public place, an *assembly.*" See the key word here? *Assembly.* Thayer gives a consensus that *ekklēsia* is an assembly of people called out from the whole, whether to meet for a public gathering (Acts 19:23-41) or as a congregation together in the first century (Acts 14:27) to give praise and worship to God.

You can look at literally every modern Bible translation where the word *ekklēsia* is used in the original Greek and you will find the word "church." The only known (to my knowledge) translator who used "congregation," the right word to be translated, was William Tyndale. Of our current translations, it is not translated assembly, or a group of individuals called out from the whole, as the original Greek intends. The issue today is that when the word church is used, it comes to define the building, not the congregation. In this book, from title to interior pages, you will note that I have not suggested we lead a

Engaging the Body

relevant *church*, but a relevant *congregation*, the *ekklēsia* Jesus promised to build, the real Body of Christ. The church as we know it in the western world is defined as the building, a specific denomination or organization, and often used to speak of the people gathered each week.

Why take three paragraphs to emphasize this? Because the congregation is a living organism, not an organization. It was designed to be a movement, never to stagnate and become a petrified organization unable to move as the *ekklēsia* did in the first century progressively. We use the word church liberally which could accurately define the organization, not the individual congregations that make up many denominational organizations. As I see it, the problem is that we have allowed too many congregations to become a church, not the *ekklēsia* as Jesus intended. Jesus didn't die for a more significant, better edifice, church building, or denominational organization and structure. He died for you and me, the gathering of people who make up the congregation, the *ekklēsia* of believers. Jesus is the head of this body, not a building or organizational structure.

Many Parts, One Body

Paul writes extensively on the gifts given to each person within the body of Christ, the congregation. It bears reading 1 Corinthians 12, but I quote parts of it here for emphasis. Paul reminds the community in Corinth, "Just as a body, though one, has many parts, but all its many parts form one body, so it is with Christ. For we were all baptized by one Spirit so as to form one body—whether Jews or Gentiles, slave or free—and we were all given the one Spirit to drink. Even so the body is not made up of one part but of many." (12-14). Each person within the congregation has a role, some significant, others appearing insignificant, all equally important. "There are different kinds of gifts, but the same Spirit distributes them. There are different kinds of service, but the same Lord. There are different kinds of working, but in all of them and in everyone it is the same God at work." (4-6)

Paul had much more to say but summarized it as this: no matter what gift a person has been given, every person within the body has been gifted to be used for serving God, living out the Great Commission, and participating in a relevant congregation. Paul provided no exceptions, "Now you are the body of

Christ, and *each one* of you is a part of it," *(emphasis mine)* (27), and neither does Jesus. The parable of the talents in Matthew 25:14-29 is a severe reminder that all who call Jesus Lord have a vital role while waiting for His soon return. No matter the size of the talent(s) given, each person is responsible for investing them for God within the congregation and community.

When we as leaders enable our members to be passive observers rather than active participants, we allow them to bury their talent. You remember what happened to the man who buried his (26-28), returning only the talent and no visible return on investment to the master when he called it in. "It was not alleged that he wasted his master's goods; he simply neglected his opportunities. Many are content to do nothing ... He who buried one talent would have buried five. His failure was in his character."[72] With that significant consequence looming for passive members of the congregation, the fundamental of equipping the congregation members becomes even more pressing. It becomes our responsibility as the under-shepherds of the Shepherd to help our members become equipped and empowered to use their Spirit-given gifts.

Equip, Empower, Engage

In congregations I have pastored, I worked with the leadership first to identify their spiritual gifts, talents, and passions, equipping them to assist others in doing the same. In preparing and implementing a strategic vision for several congregations, each chose member engagement as a crucial initiative in their path to relevancy. You know the 20/80 rule—20% of the people do 80% of the work. The 80/20 rule is also valid; 80% of the complaints come from the 20% who do little to nothing. Active members are happy members!

Numerous spiritual gifts assessments abound, but there is one I favor (at the time of this writing) for ease of use to the assessment-taker and results being sent to the individual and leadership team. Jeff Carver founded a spiritual gifts website in 2003, which I have used in numerous congregations, www.spiritualgiftstest.com. Jeff and I are casually acquainted, but I get zero monetary benefits for telling you about this resource, only the satisfaction of

---

[72] Joseph Exell, Editor, *The Bible Illustrator Commentary - Matthew* (Grand Rapids: Baker, 1978), 574

Engaging the Body

seeing how effective it is in each congregation that uses it to equip members. It is one of the best tools I have discovered and can be tailored specifically for your congregation if you choose to do so by working with Jeff and purchasing a package.

When results are sent to the individual who took the test and to leadership, it prioritizes the highest gift to the lowest. Also, which I love, each gift gets an icon. This is important as I will share in a minute. Each icon makes the gift easily identified, and each gift gets a biblical reference and how they can be used within the congregation. I must emphasize that a quality spiritual gifts assessment gives the individual an accurate assessment and backs up each gift with a biblical context. Whatever tool you choose as an assessment, please vet it well to ensure this is the case with the one selected for your congregation. When the gifts are assessed, it would be wise to enter the results with the person's information on your congregation management platform.

The next step is to find their talents. There are multiple examples of assessments available. Patrick Lencioni's, The Table Group, also developed a short but accurate assessment worth exploring, *The Working Genius*. *Working Genius* and *Strengthfinders 2.0* are very useful in helping an individual find their strengths and talents. Lastly, as it pertains to working more effectively with others as a team, I will often ask an individual to consider the DISC test. While this may seem a bit much, the results of an effectively operating congregation focused on mission, vision and relevancy cannot be overstated.

Lastly, I ask people what they are passionate about. Someone not passionate about working with children should not be shoe-horned into this slot just because they test well for it. The best intersection of individuals and service is when spiritual gifts, talents, and passions align. The successful merger of all three is what has people at the building an hour before everyone else! They are on fire for God, and their enthusiasm is contagious.

You must intentionally pour into them as a leader. Equip them with the tools they need for success. Place inexperienced individuals as apprentices with those who have experience and success. Empower leaders and their teams to work towards the stated vision and mission of the congregation. By doing so, you have an engaged congregation focused on the Great Commission, not on themselves. They are living out their purpose, and the congregation's, not their preferences.

Regarding the icons ... my leadership teams have conducted ministry fairs through various congregations I pastored. When an opportunity is listed or highlighted, the icon of the gift(s) needed in the ministry opportunity is present so people can readily match up their gifts with a need. The Ministry Placement Team puts this together as a practical resource bringing the spiritual gift assessment full circle. This Ministry Placement Team operates throughout the year to help members and new guests find places to serve and fill any open positions of need.

A Culture of Engagement

Why does engaging every member matter? "In John 17, Jesus revealed to us that the Father gives our lives to Jesus for Him to develop and teach us. For what purpose? To make us useful vessels that His Father can use to save a lost and dying world."[73] We would see more thriving and relevant congregations if leaders intentionally engaged each member in the work of God for humanity.

I would even go as far as to suggest an idea for leaders to consider. In one church I pastored, the leadership agreed to follow a specific principle. Every person who joined by baptism, profession-of-faith or transfer, had to take a spiritual gifts assessment and work with the Ministry Placement Team to find a place to serve. They would then agree to serve with excellence and distinction. Some were resistant but carried through. Others were resistant and chose not to join (they were few). This congregation embraced a culture of member engagement, and it worked. There were a few rough patches getting going, but what the leader values, the congregation soon comes to value.

Take the equipping and engagement of members and regular attendees seriously. You will find it has multiple positive consequences. More gets done. Fewer complaints come through your email or voice mail. The vision and mission become more focused and owned by individual members. Intentional discipleship is put into action through engagement. Best of all, the Great Commission gets taken seriously when all are aligned in the same direction to live out Christ's final words to the *ekklēsia*. This is the optimal living organism; one entirely relevant and changing lives through actively engaged members.

---

[73] Henry T. Blackaby, *Called and Accountable* (Birmingham: New Hope, 2005), 86

12

THE THIRD PLACE

None of the fundamentals in the development model may be as well-known, yet often ignored, as small groups; or, as I prefer to call them, *Connecting Points*, our next fundamental. Several superb books have been written on this subject over the past few years, and success rewards congregations that approach small groups purposefully and integrate them into their DNA. Using small groups of community to have significant influence is one of the vital components for a congregation that wants to be relevant. Why is that? "A deeper connection is possible through ongoing interactions, as we sit together in a small group and study scripture, share a meal, and listen to one another's stories and experiences... Small groups can provide us with the space for meaningful connection within the church ..."[74] Why is this fundamental ignored in so many congregations if implementing small groups leads to deepening relationships, intentional discipleship, and spiritual transformation?

I have observed several reasons for this from a leadership perspective. One, leadership didn't believe it was necessary, so the congregation reflected the leadership's position on small groups. Andy Stanley, the Lead Pastor of Northpoint Church in Atlanta, Georgia, and noted author, recognizes this fact. "Whenever I talk to senior pastors about their small-group ministries, I always ask about their personal small-group experience. The majority of the time—and I mean the vast majority of the time —it turns out that the pastor is not participating in a group... Groups don't have an impact on a local church

---

[74] Angela D. Schaffner, *Gather Us In: Leading Transformational Small Groups* (Nashville: Upper Room, 2020), 14.

until they become part of the church's culture. And that begins with senior leadership."[75] Truth. Members value what leaders model.

Second, it takes dedicated leaders with the gifts, talent, and passion for each small group leadership. Those individuals can be hard to identify and may be in short supply in some congregations. If the leaders are discovered, getting a time commitment can be even more difficult.

Third and perhaps the most frustrating, leaders and members do not know the ultimate purpose of small groups, or how they relate to their congregation's vision. They may not fully understand that small groups are the DNA of intentional discipleship, meaningful relationships, and effective evangelism, all of which lead to relevance. An embedded culture of small groups doesn't exist within these congregations.

Your congregation may already be doing small groups, and they were unaware of it. Each week congregations worldwide meet for studies in groups before or after their worship service. These small gatherings include studies designed to integrate biblical truth into the participant's life. Individuals gathered to discuss varying viewpoints, current life issues, and pray together. These are some of the healthy habits of effective small groups, yet there is more to be gained. Effective groups accomplish more in circles (groups) than can be accomplished in rows (worship service).

The Need for Relationships

Small groups help foster a need most humans have for relationships. Yes, some seem to prefer being alone. However, loneliness was never God's intent. Those who seem to like being alone even desire a relationship of some type. T.S. Eliot said, "There is no life that is not in community."[76] From creation, Adam recognized he was lonely and desired another with whom to have a relationship. God recognized this also; "It is not good for the man to be alone." (Genesis 2:18) Thus Eve was created as a partner to begin the bonds of community. For most humans, relationships fill an element of need within their life. "Connecting well is critical for us to experience life. Or at least life

---

[75] Andy Stanley & Bill Willits, *Creating Community* (Multnomah, Imprint of Random House, 2004, 2021), X

[76] T.S. Eliot, *"Choruses, "The Rock", Complete Poems and Plays* (New York: Harcourt & Brace, 1952), 101

The Third Place

as God intended it to be lived ... Though much has changed over the past several years, people still need community."[77]

It may take varying forms, but the need for interaction with others is still present not only in person but now through video conference and in the metaverse, or other options in the future. Community may even be considered a biblical mandate, as suggested by Angela Schaffner. "None of us is exempt from the call to be in relationships... even introverts who need a lot of downtimes... We all are included in God's call to love one another, and fulfilling that call requires interaction."[78] Community is life; life is in community.

Like me, you may have grown up with the theme song of Cheers greeting you weekly, or years since on syndicate television or current streaming platforms. You may be one of the readers too young to have ever heard this song or seen the sitcom. The lyrics apply to life today, not just a fictional bar in downtown Boston.

> "Sometimes you want to go,
> Where everybody knows your name,
> And they're always glad you came,
> You want to be where you can see,
> Our troubles are all the same,
> You want to be where everybody knows your name."

Cliff, Norm, and Frasier, among many others who gathered around Sam Malone's fictional bar, Cheers, came because they could be themselves and relate to others who accepted them with their quirks and faults. It was familiar, and they could share about life and what concerned them. I understand it was a fictional show, but it identifies a fundamental human need we all inherit; a safe place to be who we are, be fully known and yet accepted, navigate uncertain life together, and form meaningful relationships. In short, community.

Other TV shows have duplicated the concept, albeit in different settings, Friends being one of the most popular follow-up sitcoms that embraced

---

[77] Andy Stanley & Bill Willits, *Creating Community* (Multnomah, Imprint of Random House, 2004, 2021), 3

[78] Angela D. Schaffner, *Gather Us In: Leading Transformational Small Groups* (Nashville: Upper Room, 2020), 25

gathering for community at Central Perk. Whatever the sitcom, and more so in real life, we call these gathering spots the "third place." How is it best defined? "Urban planners seeking to stabilize neighborhoods are focusing on the critical role that "third places" can play in strengthening our sense of community. Third places are a term coined by sociologist Ray Oldenburg and refers to places where people spend time between home (first place) and work (second place). They are locations where we exchange ideas, have a good time and build relationships."[79] Everyone is looking for their "Cheers," a place where everyone knows their name.

Look across the landscape of your community and begin to identify the "third place" people go to away from home and outside of work. The list can continue with the bowling alley, bar, club, restaurant, lake, and campground. People drift to shared interests and hobbies. We as humans are typically drawn to the type of people who reflect us, interest us, but more importantly, accept us. The church is often left out of the preferred "third place," specifically because there is no effective community provided in small groups, one of unconditional acceptance.

Ekklēsia as Small-Groups

The early church, or assembly of believers, if you will, were small groups gathered in homes and local places. Informal, relaxed, intimate gatherings where people began and continued the process of evangelism, discipleship and supporting each other through community. While there would sometimes be larger gatherings in the synagogues, the first-century movement was built mainly on smaller groups doing community, growing together in their faith. They were also practical and service-oriented, with the needs of those less fortunate known and cared for through these gatherings.

It wasn't until the fourth century, when Constantine converted to Christianity, that small gatherings were mainly abandoned for large groups in the basilicas. The tight-knit aspect of community began to fade when this new gathering model came into being. With that change came a new host of problems, but a significant one to emerge is the realization that it is impersonal

---

[79] Stuart M. Butler and Carmen Diaz, *Third Places as Community Builders*. (https://www.brookings.edu/blog/up-front/2016/09/14/third-places-as-community-builders/), Brookings, 2016, Accessed June 15, 2022

The Third Place

and improbable to initiate and sustain relationships within a crowd. There may be small pockets within the large gathering, but they are organic, not strategic. Today we often call them cliques.

Some of the most successful church plants in North America have begun and were sustained through small groups. Saddleback Church, which Rick Warren launched in 1980, is a prime example. Today it has more than 40,000 members and 3,500+ small groups. The membership of Saddleback grew to the size it is today (not that it should be the goal) because of the culture of small groups. In 1995, Rick Warren spoke of their small groups, "We don't expect each small group to do the same things; we allow them to specialize."[80] Over the next two decades, a shift took place, creating small groups that were strategic in carrying out the five purposes of Saddleback. They differed beyond the specialty groups, with a more defined purpose: the vision of Saddleback. "Our small-groups, on the other hand, focused on individual and group health and balance ... we expect every small-group to focus on health through balancing the five biblical purposes: fellowship, discipleship, ministry, evangelism, and worship."[81], writes Steve Gladen, then pastor of small group ministry at Saddleback. Ultimately, this is what the *ekklēsia* from 1st Century to the 21st Century is: community with a purpose of connecting people and connecting to God.

"That is what God has called the church to be about: creating environments where authentic community can take place, building transformative communities where people can experience oneness with God and with one another..."[82] If your congregation does not embrace a culture of small groups, there is likely a significant gap in relationships between members and those in the community.

Perfect Alignment

Connecting points within the congregation should be made with alignment to the strategic vision, mission, and values chosen. While a specialized group may be based on a ministry activity or shared interest, it can still be

---

[80] Rick Warren, *The Purpose Driven Church* (Grand Rapids: Zondervan, 1995), 27
[81] Steve Gladen, *Small Groups with Purpose* (Grand Rapids: Baker Books, 2011), 27
[82] Andy Stanley & Bill Willits, *Creating Community* (Multnomah, Imprint of Random House, 2004, 2021), 32

connected to the vision. Small-group discipleship can focus more on the areas of the previously listed balance, creating spaces for intentional spiritual growth, service, evangelism, and fellowship. The goals for these groups are transformation, spiritual growth, and bonds with other believers.

I wrote earlier about intentional discipleship and the goal of transformation. Whether pre-decision or post-decision, the goal is a continuous journey of growth. By aligning to the fundamental of *Intentional Discipleship*, the goal is not to get a person to accept a particular belief as much as it would be for them to grow in their relationship with God. Intentional discipleship works well one-on-one and within the community provided by small groups. Stumbles happen when a person begins or continues a walk with God: a safety net is a definite need. With no support to lend a hand, doing life alone can be quite lonely and defeating. Having a support team around when a person stumbles so that the larger group can encourage, is a blessing beyond compare. Iron sharpens iron, and authentic relationships with transparency will benefit each person spiritually.

Connecting Points, seen through the lens of small groups, should be considered an integral part of the congregation's culture, eventually so firmly embedded in the DNA that it can never be pried out. This aligns perfectly with many areas of the development model, helping to develop the fundamentals through the process of community and small groups.

What Type of Small Group?

The first place to start with small groups, if they are not yet established in the congregation, is for you as the pastor or spiritual leader to create one, whether a specialty or discipleship group. Do so with an apprentice leader who will be trained to take over the next group. The second is to find more leaders and their apprentice leaders willing to start new ones. Finding leaders who put faith into practice and model the group's desired outcomes is vital. Take time to invest in these leaders and work together to set specific strategies that help identify each group's forming, sustaining, and continued success. What will be the size? What will be the focus? Specialize or Discipleship? Not to say they must remain one or the other, for a blend of up to 75% of one and 25% of another is fine, but at least know the primary focus.

Specialty groups can be varied and created for those who enjoy fishing,

The Third Place

knitting, riding motorcycles, mountain biking, water sports, single-moms, single-dads, divorcees, etc. These purposefully spiritually low-key groups invite those who would not consider themselves well-connected to God. These individuals wouldn't typically accept an invite to the worship service, may reluctantly consider a small discipleship group, but are comfortable meeting others in a like-minded third space. When a member wants to dig deeper spiritually, it can be done one-to-one, move them to an established discipleship group, or change the group from specialty to discipleship focus with everyone's permission.

Discipleship groups are teaching and spiritual growth focused. This type of group aims to interact and practice intentional discipleship. A curriculum may be chosen for each group or specific Bible study. At various times the group will connect to serve others in their community or a member in need within the congregation. The groups come together casually, building relationships, but always with the goal of intentional discipleship. This is for spiritual growth, development, and a safe place to be authentic, no matter where the person is on the journey. It is still a safe place to invite people, but they know it is a group designed for study and practical spiritual growth when they accept the invitation. Of course, the group members will periodically come together to have fun as that is part of growing healthy relationships with others.

The Practical of Small Groups

One question that often arises is how long should the group meet? Go on continuously, and people drift in and out? Set start and end dates? In my experience, the best groups operate in nine-week stretches. They may have a week or two off between the next nine-week stretch, but this gives an ideal time for those who may not want to commit to a long-term schedule. Since every congregation should be missional and focused on reaching others within the community, I recommend meshing the schedule with the local public school's quarter system. You get four nine-week quarters within a school year, with appropriate breaks for Thanksgiving, Christmas, and other intermittent days off within the school year. This also allows for a fifth group in the summer, which can be more relaxed. This format has worked successfully with congregations that have implemented it.

Curriculum and content are other critical questions. How long should a particular study or resource be used? I would again point to the nine-week cycle. Introduce new topics and study materials to change direction and keep things interesting. A best practice is for all small group leaders to meet a minimum once a quarter to determine what they will be doing for the next three to four months. This gives ample time to have all the resources available for the following defined sessions. This also keeps each group aligned and shares what works well within individual groups, so leaders learn best practices.

Where to meet? Anywhere, almost. Homes work, but today, many are reluctant to go to another's house, whom they don't already know. Meeting at the church building may prevent some from attending who object to church for personal reasons. While I wouldn't outright dismiss meetings in various homes if done correctly, the best spots for meetings are in the community. Perhaps a restaurant or favorite gathering place where some privacy can be achieved. Local libraries, or the YMCA, often have rooms that can be used for the community. A third place shouldn't be intimidating and provide a reason for a new person to reject the invite. A blend of inviting new participants to the group for the first two weeks of a new session at a neutral location is possible and practical before moving to a home. Work together with leaders and get input from those involved in attending groups. Always focus on the empty chairs, those God will bring into the circle next.

Don't be quick to dismiss online locations done through Zoom or Microsoft Team, among available platforms. While not as preferred for deeper connections, it has proved to be quite successful during the shutdowns and social distancing of COVID-19. This could be preferred for people with busy schedules during the week as they can come home, spend 45 minutes connecting and then relax without driving to and from the group. One other option will soon become a present reality: the metaverse. Already small groups are forming in the metaverse, virtual reality, having honest discussions on faith and God. It may be worth investing in some VR goggles and diving into where many people will find themselves in the future.

The last question often asked is, what should be the max attendance? I have found fifteen to be the ideal in most cases. But don't shut people out if that number is exceeded. Begin a plan to split the group and start another small group with the current apprentice leader, who will take the lead. The

The Third Place

group's current leader and new group's leader will find new apprentice leaders and continue to grow their respective groups, ready to multiply again when the time is right.

Existing Groups

Some much-needed groups exist in your community already, many of which do so anonymously but provide a ministry beyond compare. AA, NA, SA, and other Twelve-Step recovery groups serve recovering addicts who need the support of community and others who understand their addictions and recovery. I am a cheerleader for these groups and highly recommend that a congregation consider opening their church doors to these groups for use. If you don't know where to find them, reach out to the national organization and explain what the congregation would like to do. Before long, one or more groups will likely be using the building. But be warned, these are sinners. They don't smell like the "saints" and need unconditional love and acceptance—the perfect opportunity for the outward-focused, community-connected congregation!

The Why

"The health, long-term mission, and viability of the church are not going to be determined by those who gather on (the weekends). The future of the church will be determined by the depth of its disciples. People in communities through small groups… they are our future."[83] A relevant congregation will be intentional about relationships formed best by community and the connecting points provided by small groups. Be creative, name them something interesting, invite members and guests to join, or be daring and invite Twelve-Step groups to use the building.

When Rick Warren stood up in 1980, he never fully envisioned that small groups would essentially accomplish the dream of 20,000 in attendance. As a leader, you may also be wholly unprepared for what they can achieve in your congregation. Small groups serve a vital purpose of evangelism, service

---

[83] Ed Stetzer and Eric Geiger, *Transformational Groups* (Nashville: Broadman & Holman, 2014), 18

to others, intentional discipleship, and building a strong community. For the congregation to become relevant and move forward in its strategic vision, make small groups of multiple types, what I call *Connecting Points*, part of the permanent culture and DNA.

13

THE PRAYER-CENTRIC CONGREGATION

～

You may have heard the amazing music performed by the Brooklyn Tabernacle Choir as they have become world-renowned, singing in concert with some of Christian music's best-known artists. Even more fascinating than the Choir's rise to musical prominence is the story of a church that should have died but was revived by a prayer-centric pastor and congregation, both of whom did so by faith and intentionality. The story is told by the pastor who led the revitalization, Jim Cymbala, in his book, *Fresh Wind, Fresh Fire*.

Cymbala, and his wife, Carol, were experiencing frustration and burnout with the church they were called to pastor, the Brooklyn Tabernacle, in New York City. The church they took over was dying, and things were not progressing quite as hoped. Attandence was low, finances miserable, with a deacon dipping into the plate each Sunday, further reducing the meager giving. After leading the church for several years, and the ups and downs that came with leadership, Cymbala spent respite time in Florida with his in-laws to recover from a health issue and recharge. He took a day-trip deep-sea fishing in the Gulf of Mexico with the promise of further relaxation. With the sun bathing him in warmth, clear blue sky, and salty ocean, Cymbala walked to another part of the boat with fewer people around and spent time reflecting and speaking to God. Admitting his weaknesses and frustrations, pleading for a change and help from the Holy Spirit, he received an answer deep within which would change the direction of his ministry, and the Brookly Tabernacle.

"If you and your wife will lead my people to pray and call upon my name, you will never lack for something fresh to preach. I will supply all the money that's needed, both for the church and your family, and you will never have a building large enough to contain the crowds I will send in response."[84]

With that spoken to his heart, it was not long after Cymbala returned to New York City and had an opportunity to talk to his congregation for the first time since traveling to Florida. He shared his conviction and the church's future direction as led by the Holy Spirit. "From this day on, the prayer meeting will be the barometer of our church. What happens on Tuesday night will be the gauge by which we will judge success or failure because that will be the measure by which God blesses us."[85] The rest, as they say, is history: a church built on prayer that witnessed miracle after miracle within the congregation, community, and the Cymbala family. The congregation not only grew in attendance, changing locations a couple of times, but became relevant in their community.

Authored by Cymbala in 1997, *Fresh Wind, Fresh Fire*, is the story of what a congregation can do with the power of prayer. I urge you to find a copy of this book and read the powerful testimony on the pages. If it doesn't inspire you to be known as the prayer-centric congregation in your community, I am not sure what else will.

Powerless without Prayer

The fundamental of a *Prayer-Centric Congregation* may be one of the most crucial in the development model, because without prayer, not much is accomplished. I would liken it to sitting in the driver's seat of a Ferrari, wondering why this magnificent machine will go nowhere when the gas pedal is pushed to the floor. There is no need to wonder. The key isn't in the ignition, and the motor isn't running. How many individuals and congregations could say the same about their spiritual force?

As A.E. Richardson, a.k.a. The Unknown Christian, wrote a century ago, "Why are so many Christians defeated? Because they pray so little. Why are many church workers so often discouraged and disheartened? Because they pray so little ... Why are not our churches simply on fire for God? Because

---

[84] Jim Cymbala, *Fresh Wind, Fresh Fire* (Grand Rapids: Zondervan, 1997), 25
[85] Cymbala, 27

there is so little prayer ... We may be assured of this; the secret of all failure is our failure in secret prayer.[86] If our greatest failure is lack of prayer, then the greatest need is prayer, in private personally and with the congregation publicly.

Plans are made, programs developed, and vision cast, yet the congregation continues to maintain the status quo or declines each year. "Our consideration of the power and efficacy of prayer enters into the question of why we are part of a Christian congregation, and what that congregation is striving to be and do. We have to consider if we are just going around and around —like a religious merry-go-round ... Some may think the path of a religious carousel is a kind of progress, but the family of God knows better." (Tozer) [87] Is your congregation satisfied to continue its current trajectory, turning the calendar's pages to a new year with no progress or renewed outlook of growth and relevancy?

Treading the same path with the hope of different results, yet nothing changes, is that what your congregation wants? Or is there a sincere desire to become relevant and useful for God? It will take a willingness to commit to intentional prayer to achieve. But Jesus, who loves His *ekklēsia*, His congregation, of whom He is the head, has committed every resource of heaven to see congregations survive, thrive, and become relevant. Prayer unlocks the promises of God for the congregation today.

Prayer is Personal

If prayer is of such importance in the congregation's life, and the individuals who make the congregation theirs, one could argue for prayer to be a fundamental on the base of the development model. Perhaps it is so crucial as to be one of the first or second fundamentals to implement. While it might stand to reason as so, I suggest prayer that makes a difference comes from lives that have been made different through spiritual growth and vitality. A discipline of prayer is part of spiritual growth and intentional discipleship. Prayer that is powerful and reaps excellent results comes from a life connected to God. This may exist in some within your congregation currently, but intentional discipleship will infuse the need and power of prayer into even more.

---

[86] Unknown Christian, *The Kneeling Christian* (Orlando: Bridge-Logos, 2007), 8
[87] A. W. Tozer, *Prayer* (Chicago: Moody, 2016), 54

E.M. Bounds, one of the most prolific preachers and authors on prayer, writes passionately, "Praying takes it tone and vigor from the life of the man or woman exercising it. When character and conduct are at a low ebb, prayer can barely live, much less thrive."[88] We as leaders should hope for individuals in our congregations who have come to see God as their source of life and redemption, engaged in the process of discipleship. They are not perfect but trust God's amazing grace as they mature spiritually. These men and women pray with a difference, pray with power, pray with result. I have had the privilege of pastoring and attending congregations where there existed men and women who prayed with power. This only comes from a life of prayer and personal faith. Like E.F. Hutton (if you are too young to know it, look it up), when they prayed, people listened!

Those far from God cannot pray meaningful prayers that move mountains, as Jesus promised (Mathew 21:21). Yes, God hears their prayers when they cry out, for He never turns His ear from those He loves, but they are simple prayers for assistance and an appeal for grace and mercy. As the person leans in on God, experiencing Him personally, their character shifts, as do their prayers. We as spiritual leaders should be speaking of personal prayer often and its importance in daily life. To "pray without ceasing" (1 Thessalonians 5:17) is to teach each person how to pray, why to pray, and the necessity of prayer in the life of every believer. Any personal relationship to grow requires communication between two individuals, should prayer be any different?

Such it is with God—for prayer is communication with Him on a personal basis. "Prayer is the opening of the heart to God as to a friend."[89] We engage in this conversation of prayer by faith that God hears, a significant part of spiritual development and a discipline of discipleship.

Practicing What We Preach

How can any pastor or spiritual leader within a congregation encourage others to pray when they do not have a prayer life that makes a difference? It is "blind leading the blind" in this regard, teaching on theory, not of practice. There is only so long we can go without prayer in our spiritual lives before it becomes evident to the congregation. Preaching suffers, as does leadership

---

[88] E.M. Bounds, *E.M. Bounds on Prayer* (New Kensington: Whitaker House, 1997), 553

[89] E.G. White, Steps to Christ: *With Historical Introduction and Notes by Denis Fortin* (Berrien Springs: Andrews University Press, 2017), 263

effectiveness. The congregation may become stagnant due to the absence of prayer in the lives of its leaders. If a leader doesn't believe in prayer, practice prayer, or see marked and evident results from prayer, why should anyone being led by this leader expect supernatural results within the congregation?

Perhaps the most remarkable book on prayer I have ever read, as it applies to the pastor and spiritual leaders of a congregation, is *Power Through Prayer*, by the afore mentioned E.M. Bounds. Bounds was a preacher, having served as a chaplain during the Civil War and as a minister to various congregations until his death. He was known as *the* man of prayer. Only one who knows the power of prayer can write to others and challenge them to engage in the same. His challenge to spiritual leaders is more urgent today than when he wrote, "What the church needs today is not more or better machinery, not new organizations or more and novel methods. She needs men (and women) whom the Holy Spirit can use, men of prayer, men mighty in prayer."[90] Leaders attend conferences to draw lessons from other leaders. They hear of best practices, who has done what, with all credit given to the method or successful leader. God desires to give credit to the man or woman who leads by prayer. It is our most potent weapon, yet the least used.

I will be the first to admit that I have so much more to learn about the power of prayer in my own spiritual life and leadership. I am ever striving to make prayer a most critical work. Yet like most, I allow it to become a "back-burner" practice due to what I perceive to be urgent issues that need to be dealt with. Slowly this thick-skulled person is learning that most issues and challenges are best dealt with in prayer, seeking the wisdom, knowledge, and insight of the Holy Spirit.

I have seen first-hand what congregations can accomplish when I, as the leader, bathe everything in personal, private prayer. I have seen the converse, where my prayer life has been lacking, leading the congregation to become stagnant and impotent. I am humbled and refreshed to know prayer makes a difference and equally frustrated with myself when I let prayer become an afterthought in my ministry.

Imagine if your private prayer life grew to the capacity God desires, and what He could do through your leadership. Spiritual leaders who pray lead spiritual congregations that pray.

---

[90] *Bounds*, 468

The Praying Congregation

Through experience, I have concluded that the most relevant congregations are those which make personal and public prayer a priority. It isn't a "When all else fails, pray," outlook, but one that makes seeking God in prayer a top priority. People attend worship services when they know prayer is powerful and effective and reaches the throne of God. Just as in the story of the Brooklyn Tabernacle Choir, people attend because they know what results from a congregation that pursues prayer.

Sadly, many lead the congregation in public prayer and rarely bow their head in private. Every meeting that involves decisions and planning is met with minimal prayer for God's leading and guidance. I have seen these token prayers; I have prayed them. Most often, plans are made, programs developed, and a follow-up request for God to bless the decisions is made. If Christ is the head of the church, should it not stand to reason that we ask first in prayer what God would lead the congregation to do?

"For the true Christian, the one supreme test for the present soundness and ultimate worth of everything religious must be the place our Lord occupies in it."[91] These final written words of Tozer before he died should be another reason we pursue prayer as it relates to the life of the congregation and leader. We should do nothing without placing the decision before God in prayer, seeking wisdom far beyond our own. From small congregations to large faith-based organizations, every decision should be made united with persistent prayers.

The prayer meeting has become a relic of the past in most congregations, but perhaps it's time for a revival. I have been observing the past two years as prayer groups are thriving through use of technology, conference calls, and video conferencing top the list. People are beginning to appreciate that praying together is powerful. When the answers to prayer are shared in follow-up meetings, it emboldens people to pray more and expect results. All are witness to, "A prayer of a righteous person, when it is brought about, can accomplish much." (James 5:16)

---

[91] A.W. Tozer, *The Waning Authority of Christ in the Church*. (https://www.awtozerclassics.com/articles/article/4938678/86408.htm.) Accessed June 3, 2022

The Prayer-Centric Congregation

As Pastor Cymbala chose to let prayer meetings be the measuring stick of success in his church, perhaps prayer meetings in person or online will become your congregation's metric also. It may start small, but if a few are committed, especially the congregation's leaders, others will begin to see the value and results of prayer and join in. What a moment it will be when others outside the church walls come to know your congregation as the one who prays with results! Powerful witness indeed!

"The life, power, and glory of the church is prayer… Without it, the church is lifeless and powerless… The life of its members is dependent on prayer."[92] If prayer is made a fundamental of your congregation, it will bleed into the lives of every member and the community as well. I urge you to find ways to exhibit the value of meaningful prayer in the life of your congregation, from children's ministry to senior-age ministry.

Final Thoughts on Prayer

I have quoted and shared more on prayer as I am passionate about the power and results of prayer. As a spiritual leader, it is your lifeblood. No matter how qualified a leader may be, what they can accomplish for God will be nothing significant without prayer. Why? "God's leaders are preeminently men (and women) of prayer."[93] Consider this; could you imagine Moses leading the Israelites without a connection to God? Nehemiah rebuilding the walls? Daniel leading a heathen nation by example? Joseph rising to the second in command of all of Egypt? Esther standing for her people before the king? Biblical examples of powerful leadership exhibit men and women who communicated with God. In each, the vital connection was the power of prayer. And of any who could have gotten by without prayer, Jesus was in private prayer daily, seeking connection with His Father, and guidance to follow His will.

Look at the history of Christianity and those who got results for God; Dwight Moody, Martin Luther, William Carey, H.M.S. Richards, Mark Finley, Hannah Smith, C.D. Brooks, Charles Spurgeon, Hudson Taylor, and Billy Graham, to name a few. Each was powerful in result because they were mighty

---

[92] E.M. Bounds, *E.M. Bounds on Prayer* (New Kensington: Whitaker House, 1997), 185
[93] Bounds, 57

in prayer. Forego the next leadership conference and church growth seminar to focus your time on personal spiritual growth and connecting with God in powerful, private prayer.

I also advise purchasing the E.M. Bounds compilation on prayer, which I have quoted here. Seven of his best books on prayer, all in one. You will never view prayer the same again, that I can promise you. The difference in your leadership, preaching, and congregation will become the testimony to prayer as a powerful agent. Other pastors and leaders will come to you, and your congregation, to observe the pattern of success to be duplicated. But, you will know it wasn't methods, plans, or programs that made the difference. It was prayer.

14

Nuts and Bolts of Relevancy

Much like the proverbial sausage in the factory, how things are done isn't as inspiring as the finished product. Few want to take the time to invest in preparing and planning for the outcome, but it is this important work that allows the latter to be done well. This chapter falls into the category of not flashy but necessary. These "nuts and bolts" which keep a church together and operating at efficiency are two fundamentals, *Finance and Facility* and *Programs and Processes*. Some within your congregation will have the spiritual gifts and natural talents with the accompanying passions to connect with these areas and will help the congregation due to their willingness to be involved behind the scenes.

I venture to say many congregations have ineffective programs and outcomes, from inside ministries to outside ministries, worship services, teaching ministries, and so much more, due to lack of sufficient planning and organizational purpose. The future health of these four fundamental areas stems from the *Strategic Vision* fundamental, because these fundamentals are best defined by the roadmap and destination the congregation will adopt. Yet these necessary fundamentals find even further advancement when discipleship, prayer, communication, leadership development, visitations, and sermons have been defined, emphasized, and become important. Why the facility should be beautiful takes on new importance when seen in the light of worship and community engagement.

While they may be time-consuming to initially set up, processes become essential in decision-making and follow-through, advancing the church's overall strategy. Finances are a crucial component, yet they will never be an issue, in my sincere opinion, when they align with intentional discipleship and become parallel with vision. The right programs become evident when internal and external demographics are considered.

These four areas will not pause when you enter the congregation for the first time as a leader or attempt to change the course of the congregation through revival and redirection. They must be monitored as you progress, but they will slowly become adjusted to align with the desired outcome of the congregation, which is fulfilling the vision, and being relevant. In many congregations, these four areas are the "master," driving decisions and hindering the work. In a congregation moving forward with vision and desired relevance, these four areas will soon become the "servant," enhancing and adding to the work and desired outcomes. As tedious as they may be, they stand essential, nonetheless. How can these four areas add to your congregation's vision and purpose? Make them a spiritual necessity, not just a needed function.

Finances: Giving

As congregation leaders, we are familiar with the biblical truth of tithing, a tenth of all God has graciously given. Throughout the history of the Old Testament and New, tithe and other offerings are a component of worship and gratitude. When it is made to be an obligation or a checklist item in the life of a Christian, it becomes wearisome rather than a blessing. Few things upset people more or keep guests from returning, as when the pastor or congregational leaders start putting their hand in the purse of the person or family. This is exhibited when standing up each week and a call for giving is put forth urgently such as pressing for money to accomplish projects or retire debt. The deficit in giving as compared to the budget is listed in the bulletin or weekly email. A series on stewardship is presented which happens to correspond with a severe dip in giving within the congregation. Then there is the phone call or visit from the pastor to the parishioner to have a private conversation on their giving, or lack of, in the previous months. Challenging them to "get right with God through giving."

Nuts and Bolts of Relevancy

Giving is intensely personal. Yes, giving tends to reflect the relationship with God a person is experiencing. Some will give regardless, for they feel it their duty as if their eternal outcome depends on it. But most give for multiple reasons. First, they give back to God with a sense of gratitude. This continues as they experience God more personally through discipleship. I have seen giving increase within a congregation when the congregation's spirituality was trending upward. Giving is a spiritual matter.

The second reason people give is for purpose. There may be a tenth that is "required" of them biblically, but often those giving will open their wallets or purses for a defined purpose and outcome. They sense God doing amazing work in the life of their congregation, and there is a clearly defined mission to be fulfilled. They sense and observe all of this, and the Holy Spirit prompts them to give more. In times past, they may have sensed an obligation to give, yet neglected to do so believing the money would just disappear, used unwisely, assisting the church in wandering around in circles with no clear future. No one likes to give to a deficit of poor spending and unwise budget habits. But give them a clear-cut purpose with a decisive outcome and watch the giving trend upwards in a profound way.

Author J. Cliff Christopher agrees and explains how giving is approached within most congregations. "The biggest problem I still see in our churches is that we talk way too much about the need for money and not about the ministry being done. We talk about maintaining rather than transforming. We do not help our people to see how they can invest in changing lives but rather how they are supporting an institution."[94]

The third reason people often give is a story—not just any story, mind you, but the story of a life impacted due to the generosity and giving of people to make a particular program, event, or similar, happen. Perhaps it was an evangelistic endeavor. A community-based Vacation Bible School outside the church. Prison ministry, homeless ministry, children of single parents, or down the list. There are fewer compelling reasons to give than the true, unpolished story of a person who gave their life to God due to a ministry, outreach endeavor, or program. Isn't that why we exist? A relevant congregation makes a spiritual impact in the lives of those within the church and without, and it takes funds to accomplish it. I have never seen powerful stories hinder giving. I have seen personal giving skyrocket for a specific need when the power of story is

---

[94] J. Cliff Christopher, The Church Money Manual (Nashville: Abingdon Press, 2014), 27

harnessed with need. These are not stories to manipulate people into giving; please never abuse them. These stories show that the money has been and will be invested in bringing an eternal return on the generous gifts of others.

God's people are naturally inclined to give, especially those who are growing as intentional disciples. They won't need to be coerced, visited, guilted, or any other tactic used by leaders in the past to increase giving. Provide opportunities online, through their phone, and when they arrive in the building weekly. Share the vision, tell the story, and watch the giving go up as a result of lives impacted!

Finances: Stewardship

Every congregation must use the gracious gifts of its members and attendees with wisdom and stewardship. It begins with the pastor and leaders of the congregations setting an example. There should be a resistance to extravagant spending that benefits one or two people, done under the guise of being the "Lord's servant." Authentic spiritual leadership will reject this thinking outright. I am still amazed, and angered, by spiritual leaders that financially abuse and manipulate their members and supporters.

The budget and priorities of the congregation should well-reflect the purpose and vision, which, if done correctly, will be one centered on the mission and the gospel to as many people as possible within the congregation and community. When a full strategic vision is in place, those on the designated finance team (yes, you should have one) will have no problem determining where and when money should be directed. Every expenditure should easily align with the congregation's voted vision, mission and values.

There ought to be complete transparency of the financial state of the congregation to anyone who asks and upon review at every leadership team/board meeting. Every penny is accounted for with accuracy and wisdom. Once or twice a year, a review of finances should be offered to the church in a separate meeting away from the day of worship. Allow individuals to see how the funds have been used, and the stories told as a result of wise budgeting and spending.

Wise pastors and leaders will consider a couple of things: put together a finance team of spiritual men and women who understand the church's vision and desired outcome well. It is not necessary to chair the team but find an exceptional person to do so. A plus is that each member of the team has a working understanding of accounting principles, budgets, and economics. This will create a highly functional finance team that provides guidance, oversight, and accountability.

Personally, as a leader have no access to the church's finances, EVER—I can't emphasize this enough! Don't have a checkbook, debit card, or anything which allows temptation to manifest itself. Do not put your signature on any document that would allow you access to church funds. Many a pastor has surrendered their ministry due to financial impropriety. It is one of the devil's key areas to undermine a pastor's calling. Every reimbursement should be spelled out as to why the expenditure was made, what was purchased, and for what reason. It's not to give the finance team and leadership board control but to exercise prudence and servant leadership. Consider rejecting, with gratitude, any financial gift a member or the congregation wants to give you. Obviously, there are some exceptions, such as pastor's appreciation, and when you leave the congregation, but for the most part steer clear.

Ask the same of department leaders as you would ask of yourself and the top leaders of the congregation regarding financial integrity. Every year there should be training on budget, expenses, and how each department leader will use their funds. Consider setting up a quarter system of budget allocation to avoid those leaders who wait until month twelve to spend all their annual allotted budget. Every leader is accountable for wise spending and use. If they are not willing to do so, then it may be time to find another leader for that ministry or program.

Congregations and faith-based organizations that exercise prudent financial control will see an increase, especially when they are transparent. Finances don't control the congregation; they assist in fulfilling the vision and mission when used correctly. Finances are a necessary component to the congregation and should be embraced as stewardship resources from God.

Facilities: First Impressions

When guests arrive for the first time at the building where your congregation meets, they will see and notice things those who have attended for an extended period will never notice. I pastored a congregation a few years ago which had been in their building twenty years before my arrival. From the original construction to my arrival, the traffic patterns had dramatically increased on the road the church was built near, giving significant exposure every day. When people drove by or came into the parking lot, they encountered potholes, cracks, weeds, faint parking lines, and no guest parking. Throughout the building excess wear was evident. When I brought it up to others, they realized they had become so accustomed to it that they never noticed it any longer.

I did. I am also confident most guests did as well. The building was being constructed in multiple phases, which had been broadly extended over time due to lack of resources. The sanctuary also served as a fellowship hall. There were enormous stains on the carpet from prior meals, quite noticeable when one sat during for the worship service or then kneeled on them for prayer. Before long, as part of the congregation's strategic vision, the entire facility was renovated, and significant changes took place outside in the parking lot, landscaping, as well as the complete interior. They determined to be a welcoming church for those seeking God in their voted mission. They also realized the community they resided in would probably not tolerate a building in disrepair and might do a U-turn once they hit the parking lot. The facility, as they realized, was a hindrance to many who made assumptions about the congregation based on the appearance of the building.

Changes were prominent. The first one was for guests. Before the renovation, the best parking spots were within 100 feet of the front door—everyone who arrived at the building first parked in the prime locations. When guests arrived, they were left to find parking spots elsewhere. With the changes came signage that included a warm welcome to guests when they pulled into the driveway, with arrows pointing to parking for guests, families with children, and senior citizens.

One positive of guest parking within sight of the front door was the greeter's awareness of new people coming in, ready to smile and welcome them to the congregation. The difference was felt as time went by. The facilities were beautiful, and effort was made to keep them that way. Guests had positive impressions from the entrance through to the bathrooms. Yes, never underestimate the condition of the bathroom, the one place women will often decide if they want to remain in the congregation or not. Seriously!

Nuts and Bolts of Relevancy

Facilities: Challenges and Obstacles

I have been with differing congregations and observed many others, who were aware, most of the time, of the current conditions of their building, but unable to get the needed funds to begin the changes necessary. I have always told them it is easier than they think. Most are daunted by the task and shy away from it. Continuing to exist in a run-down, unwelcoming building does not represent the excellence that God deserves, nor the community you seek to invite in.

I grew up attending two different churches within our denomination and loved both. To this day, each looks like they did when I was in elementary school more than forty years ago. One has the same carpet and colors—forty-five years later! It is kept clean, but it is not modern and relevant to those who come to visit. The other church building is deteriorating, with the same or worse conditions of the past forty years. When one drives into the parking lot for the first time, their initial instinct may be to continue to the exit without stopping. The outside of the facility is aged, parking lot and curbing is in neglect, and old playground equipment in disrepair quite evident. I know I have been tempted to pass through, yet I park anyways and go inside when I am occasionally back in town to visit.

The primary challenges and obstacles to changing the state of the facilities are money, desire, and lack of clear vision. As I have said previously, most don't even pay attention to the facility's current condition because they are accustomed to it. The general feeling is often, "I come here, I am happy, why change?" They don't care about improving much. Others sense that the building needs repairs and renovations to fix issues and update the aesthetics, but it isn't a burden to them. They feel that anyone genuinely seeking truth doesn't care about the building. Still, others focus on the limitations of finance, while some don't understand the purpose and need of facilities that exhibit beauty and excellence.

In an interview once, I was asked what I would do with small churches within our denominations that were small in attendance and buildings were becoming worn, and frankly an embarrassment in their community. Growing up in the Midwest in a farming community, I said the first thing that came to my mind, "I'd take them out behind the barn and shoot them." The reaction on some of the faces of those in the interview was priceless. My wife pointed out that was the moment I lost the job! I did go on to express myself further. I stated it would be better for those congregations to close their church, sell the building to a congregation who could keep it up, and either gather in small groups elsewhere, or rent from the next owner of the building. I believe that ugly, run-down, out-of-date buildings are a poor reflection of God and a congregation's commitment to God. If you don't think the beauty of the place God's people come to each week matters, take time to read the account of the sanctuary prepared by Moses in the wilderness and the later temple built by Solomon.

The obstacle of why and how is overcome by a strong strategic vision, accompanied by mission for outreach and relevance in the community. When reaching others is a priority and purpose of the body of Christ, other things that seemed impossible to do in the past become probable and possible in the present. Within the last several years, I have assisted two congregations in completely renovating their facilities. They updated and modernized in every way possible, reflecting a beauty and excellence never experienced before. The best part was that each renovation was completed debt-free, with all the money being raised for the projects, most coming from within the congregation, some from others outside the congregation. There was soon an evident appreciation from guests and returning members, which further affirmed to even the doubters the necessity of the renovation.

How did this happen? The facilities were seen as vital in accomplishing a clearly communicated vision and mission for the congregation. Members began to see and fully understand the importance of beauty in the facility that reflected excellence, honored God, and welcomed people who would visit. The facilities were practical and enabled programs to be done well. One of the most significant aspects of each renovation was the addition of gathering space to build relationships and community. As I write this, I am amazed at how people who had not previously cared gave so generously to see the facilities improved.

One last quick note for those in buildings that look dated due to architectural and design style. There isn't much that can be done about the outdated design style from an exterior or interior standpoint, without a major costly renovation, but that doesn't excuse beauty and excellence from still being important. Consider having a designer come in and give some new updated cues that allow the building to look more present in the 21st Century. Small touches can work well, and the right color palette can improve design as well.

Nuts and Bolts of Relevancy

But, How?

Don't know where to start? It's incredible what a five-gallon bucket of paint, in a carefully chosen neutral color palette, can accomplish. Paint is the least expensive way to inspire that I have found in twenty years of updating and renovating church facilities. Consider starting at the point of entrance and maximum impact on guests. Find other creative ways to adopt some beautification without spending much money. The results will come through immediately. Giving has always followed once people see the possible and the purpose for the changes.

In one congregation pastored years ago, there was serious doubt about where the money could be found for the urgent renovation needed in the sanctuary and foyer. The 1970s décor wasn't looking too good in the 2000s! There was $5,000 available of the $40,000 needed for aesthetic updates. I challenged the leadership team to transform the foyer as a surprise to the congregation. They began the project within two weeks and completed it between two weekends. When people walked in for the services after the renovation, some gasped. One such couple approached me after the service and asked how much it cost to renew the sanctuary completely. $35,000 was the amount budgeted, which I told them. On the following Tuesday, I had a check for $35,000. Two months later, a dedication of a wholly transformed sanctuary took place.

How Processes Bring Success

I won't spend as much time on processes, but I will say they are essential. If you have processes for follow-up with guests, ministering to children, and reaching the community, I suggest they be refined and used every week. It would seem a strong statement that processes can bring success, but they do. As Nick Saban tells his players, "Stick to the process, and the outcomes will take care of themselves." Processes require discipline, and some in your congregation have the mindset, gifts, talent, and passion for making processes work. Use those talents.

What is meant by a process? Let me give you an example. In most congregation, when a guest arrives, they are asked to sign a guest card or guest book. What typically happens to that information? Nothing. Now I know there are some congregations, and maybe yours is one of them, that will follow up with them, eventually. The problem is that it is too late when they receive a note,

Leading a Congregation to Relevance

email, or phone call. Church growth experts, of which there are many, suggest guests need to hear from the congregation they visited within seventy-two hours of their initial visit. After that, the percentage of a second visit drops significantly. What process could help with guest retention and lead to full assimilation?

Using Planning Center Online, or similar management tools allows congregations to set up a process that can bring significant success in turning guests into the church family. It works like this:

1. The greeter makes initial contact and asks the individual(s) if this is their first visit to the church. If so, they're told with enthusiasm how happy the congregation is to have them and asked if the guest might share a couple of pieces of information with the congregation. If the guests say yes, which they typically will when greeted warmly, then...
2. The greeter has an iPad or similar tablet with Planning Center Online operating. They simply hit the "+" sign to add a new person and begin entering their first and last name, phone number, and email. Leave the address to later; you don't want to overwhelm them at first. If there are multiples in the family, sort out spouse, kids, etc. When the individual inputting the information hits enter to save, it triggers a pre-arranged process, which...
3. Sends a message to the guest assimilation team that there was a new guest and then initiates a task for the team. The task of the individuals on the guest team at that point is to send an email within twenty-four hours of the visit with a warm greeting thanking the guest for their visit, including a digital gift card for Starbucks, or similar, as a thank you gift. The email will contain the church website address, an invitation to join the newsletter list, and encourage a return visit. Attached also is a redemption code for a special gift for those who come a second time. When this task is completed, it is now time for the pastor who...
4. Will get a task request to follow up with the guest by making a phone call on the third day after their visit. This call is a simple thank you for attending, asking if there is anything the pastor can do for the individual/family, and encouraging them to return. They may also suggest the guests accept texts and email by signing up for church updates. This is the end of the task process, but more is still to come.

Nuts and Bolts of Relevancy

When the guest returns a second time, which is easy to identify due to the incentive included in the email, which they now turn in, the greeter marks them as present. This triggers a new process, which is different from the first but shows the one who visited again they are valued and appreciated. This is the significance of a process followed with discipline and utilizing spiritual gifts and talents within the congregation. Some processes can be set up for efficiency, continued growth, and relevancy.

Setting up various processes as needed within the congregation can be time-consuming at first, but save much time, energy and potential conflict in the future. When processes are identified and implemented it releases valuable time for more important issues to be dealt with, and aids in higher-functioning ministry outcomes. Lastly, they can be used very effectively for strengthening relationships and intentional discipleship, ones not to be overlooked.

Programs

Programs are not what is presented each week when people come to the service but are considered ministry in action to children and youth, young adults, and older. Any program should clearly define why it exists and its alignment with the congregation's ultimate purpose. Many a congregation has programs they are proud of, but not all contribute much to accomplishing the church's mission.

I once joined the pastoral team of a church that had eighty-four programs when I arrived. They were proud of their programs and referred to this number often as a barometer of their commitment to ministering. After two-plus years of digging further, it became clear many of the programs consumed money and resources but accomplished little else. As the congregation began to define its mission and vision, with a clear strategy for accomplishing both, several the programs were discontinued. I suggest to congregations often that it is better to support fewer programs with excellence than have more with pervading mediocrity and less involvement.

Often people will approach the pastor, or leaders within the congregation, with a wonderful idea the congregation should undertake as a new program or ministry. I typically ask them a series of questions.

1. *You have the dream, see a need, and are you ready to lead?*
2. *How does this proposed program align with the strategic vision?*

3. Is this a short-term or long-term proposed program?
4. If short-term, what are the proposed parameters of time?
5. If long-term, what metrics of success will be in place?
6. Do you have a proposed "apprentice leader" you will develop?
7. If not on the leadership team, who will mentor from the team?
8. What is your preferred outcome for the proposed program?
9. How do you propose to fund the program for the next 18 months?

These questions help the person who comes to the leader with a proposed new program to think it through. Any proposed program should align with the strategic vision voted on and assist with the outcomes of the congregation overall. I have had to gently tell people "No" in the past when the questions answered were not affirmative, for the proposed program did not align with the congregation's strategic vision. "No" is hard: "Yes" is easy. But saying "yes", and observing resources depleted in other programs, or a new program failing due to a lack of accountability, dying from lack of funding, or leadership burnout, is even more challenging. I am not suggesting that a new program should never be started. A congregation's leadership team should put parameters in place to determine if a program is to be launched and use additional processes to evaluate the programs currently in place.

Programs exist from mid-week to weekend services, children's ministry, and homeless ministry. Each should have clearly defined parameters with metrics to measure the program's success or lack thereof. I have heard many times from a former church leader, "What we value, we evaluate." I have said it already in this book; we measure what we treasure. Data can drive adjustments, affirm decisions to support ongoing work within the program, or compel a decision to change directions. The preliminary determination for the need and purpose of each program and the place it occupies within the congregation should be this: does the program help the congregation become relevant in the lives of others? Does it align with the voted strategic vision, mission, and desired outcome?

Every Nut and Bolt Matters

You can have a beautiful automobile that can still be flawed when a nut or bolt is not securely fastened or missing. Try driving tomorrow with lug nuts

Nuts and Bolts of Relevancy

loose on one wheel and see how far you get. Don't underestimate the negative impacts of the nuts and bolts, identified here as finance, facilities, processes, and programs, when they are not functioning well, or tightened down by processes and measurements.

These two fundamentals stem from the *Strategic Vision* fundamental, but also succeed when other fundamentals are strengthened. People within your congregation have the gifts to make these areas function well, and with prayer and spiritual gifts testing, you will find them. Their talents will bring success to these areas. Additionally, it will benefit the congregation as it begins to fulfill the mission and vision decided upon, strengthened through the nuts and bolts which are necessary to congregational relevance.

15

Embracing Guests

Any congregation's continued growth and influence comes from the infusion of new people. Yet knowing this, many congregations are less-than-welcoming to guests. I have personally been a guest that felt unwelcome when visiting another congregation. In one such visit, numerous people walked by me in the hallway and sanctuary without saying hello or extending a hand. I sat alone in the pew, and not once during the service or after did anyone come and speak to me other than the pastor and a person I already knew. Not surprisingly, this congregation made a point of being known as a "friendly congregation."

I am not faulting the congregation I visited. As a pastor for two decades, I have witnessed what happens when a congregation is not focused on welcoming guests. There also have been times I absent-mindedly walked by a guest without saying a word, only to hear about it later. It takes a disciplined and conscious effort to welcome guests who venture in the doors, offering unconditional hospitality to everyone. It must be integrated into the culture, communicated often, and lived out by the leaders. This is possible for the congregation willing to give weight to the fundamental of *Guest Integration*. Guests are not there on a whimsical visit but by divine appointment. What they experience upon arrival at your building will determine many things for them, not just if they will return for future visits.

Embracing Guests

Hospitality

When this word is considered, most people will relate it to a service-related industry—restaurants and hotels come to mind. In these cases, hospitality is the experience a guest enjoys when they visit. A pleasant experience that overwhelms them will lead to subsequent visits and sharing their experience with others. A poor experience will ensure they never come back but will share their negative encounter with others. Sadly, in many congregations today, hospitality is absent. There is no consideration for what a guest experiences when arriving for the first time.

Authors Jason Young and Jonathan Palm make a very persuasive argument for how hospitality should be viewed within the congregation. "Hospitality can't just be a job title at your church. It's not just the team's job to provide hospitality to new guests. Instead, it needs to be a cultural element of your church. A shared value... When something becomes part of the culture in your organization, there is clarity and understanding. It's seen in everything and everyone"[95] The last sentence is the key; "everything and everyone" models the culture of hospitality for it to be successful.

Let's get honest here. Have you ever pastored or led in a congregation where it is challenging to find people who want to greet on the weekend for services? Maybe they volunteered and are scheduled, but some don't show up or find something else to do? It would be evident that the culture of hospitality isn't present. There have been some mornings I walked into the foyer of one congregation I pastored and saw no one standing at the door, and any information to be handed out was lying on the table. If I were a guest that day, I would have been highly tempted to do an immediate U-turn and head to another church down the street. I would also share my experience with others so they would be forewarned.

Perhaps the opposite has occurred in your congregation. There is a great hospitality environment and team in place. Warm, smiling faces at the door each weekend, ready to offer guests a welcome they have never experienced before. The team has thought it through to the end of the service. That is until members disappear within ten minutes, and guests are left to wonder if they were the last ones left behind. Perhaps even worse, while the guests were present, not many of the members came up to welcome them and invite them

---

[95] Jason Young & Jonathan Malm, *The Comeback Effect* (Grand Rapids: Baker Books, 2018), 34, 35

to be part of the activity they were currently involved in or going to next. For guests to be welcomed thoroughly, the culture of hospitality needs to extend throughout the congregation, from young to old.

Young and Malm suggest four identifiers for a congregation with hospitality embedded in its culture. "It's pervasive, it's an identity, it's valued from the top down, it's valued with resources."[96] Reflect right now on these four measurement areas as they relate to your congregation. Could your congregation answer affirmatively on all four? Three? Two? Don't be disappointed if you can't find the answer you desire, it takes time. That is why *Guest Integration* is higher up in the development model: a culture of discipleship and personal connections are vital for a culture of hospitality to take hold as part of the congregation's DNA.

Note, lest you think hospitality is just for hotels, restaurants, and other fine businesses that attract customers for profit, it isn't. It's a biblical mandate. Paul admonished the Romans to "Seek to show hospitality." (Romans 12:13). The writer of Hebrews, whom most think is Paul, wrote, "Do not neglect to show hospitality to strangers, for thereby some have entertained angels unawares." (13:2). Lastly, Peter admonishes his readers to "Show hospitality to one another without grumbling." (1 Peter 4:9). However, in the next verse, Peter states why the reader should show hospitality, and why we still do so for the guests that arrive within our congregation. "As each has received a gift, use it to serve one another, as good stewards of God's varied grace." (4:10)

Each of us has experienced grace and redemption, intentionally begun a journey of growth in our relationship with God and all that experience gives us. Hospitality within the congregation is giving that gift of grace to others when they arrive. No matter who they are, what they look like, or what they believe. We are called to extend the gifts freely given to us, passed on to them through acts of genuine kindness, acceptance, and grace. A culture of hospitality reminds members that it is an honor to share with others what has been so graciously given to them.

The Guest Experience

What a guest experiences when they arrive starts at the entrance to the parking lot. This has been mentioned in another chapter, but a reminder of how

---

[96] *Young & Malm*, 36

important the aesthetics and grounds of the church facility can be for a guest. They see what members have gotten used to seeing and now overlook. Is the parking lot clearly marked, or not? Severe cracks and potholes? Are directional signs inviting guests to their parking spots close to the front entrance, or are they left to find their own space? Is the landscaping manicured and inviting? Is the building well-maintained and representative of its community, or even a step above? All of this can make an impression on a new guest, and in some cases, might prevent them from exiting their car.

When guests arrive, are they greeted by someone in the parking lot before entering the building? I have seen it done in a very informal way using two greeters just standing in the parking lot, near the guest parking, talking casually. When the guest exits their car and looks around, these greeters say hello, welcome them, and point them to the front door. This is a very casual way of greeting new people without intimidating them. I have also experienced a golf cart coming right up to the vehicle and a smiling driver inviting the guest to take a quick ride to the front door. The driver asks their names and drops them off at the door with a smile.

And a random thought; have lots of umbrellas handy for those rainy days, keeping your guests dry from their car to the front door. Don't underestimate what that simple act will do for the guests who experience it firsthand!

What will the guest find when they walk in the front door? Hopefully, a smiling face who already knows their name. Why? The driver in the golf cart whispered it on their radio after they dropped the guest off at the door, making the initial welcome much more personal. You know how you feel when someone knows your name and uses it. We get this service at some of the best hotels and restaurants. Why not for our guests at church? When welcomed, the guests are asked to share brief information to be entered into the chosen management platform, which initiates a continued follow-up over the next few days. Then the greeter takes them to the appropriate areas based on who is visiting and shows them briefly around the church, so they find the restrooms, classrooms, and primary service location.

This is more than many congregations may already be doing. Yet this is programmed hospitality from a team of individuals who want the experience to be the best possible for the guest. What about the rest of the leaders and members? For hospitality to work to its highest level within the congregation, it must be a culture embedded in everyone and everything, remember? What

Leading a Congregation to Relevance

will that look like if deeply ingrained within the congregation's culture? From leaders to members, how would that be exhibited to guests as they move from the entrance to join current programs or services throughout the building?

I suggest a couple of things: first, if a guest is invited to join a study class before the main service, always have empty chairs available when they arrive in the classroom. A class with no empty chairs is uncomfortable for guests and often draws unwanted attention. It could even suggest that others are not invited. The leader and members of each class should be aware each week of who might arrive for the first time, ready to make them feel invited without being overwhelmed. Empty chairs, preferably a minimum of two together for couples, are a simple invitation to participate.

With all the social pressures that come with it, children and youth have an even more significant obstacle to entering new spaces than adults. Leaders of each class and specific students in each respective class can become purposefully aware of how new guests will be welcomed into the class when they arrive, making even the children of new guests appreciate their experience in the congregation. The experience of a child visiting for the first time is often overlooked and can be a significant determiner as to whether the parents will make a return visit in the future.

Then there is church service. Having individuals within the main auditorium welcoming guests is a pleasant experience, and they can assist with seating also. I have witnessed designated guest seating—subtly marked— scattered throughout the auditorium, which does two things. First, it guarantees seats for the guests. Second, members know that most often, if someone is sitting in those marked spots, they are guests and should be welcomed warmly. This is a subtle process for making guests feel included and continues to keep hospitality at the forefront of the members' minds. During the service, don't ask guests to stand up. Even meet and greet can be uncomfortable for guests as members stand up while they remain seated; often, they are unsure what to do during this time. The pre-selected seating arrangements for guests in pre-chosen areas allows those around them to greet them naturally, without guests feeling uncomfortable.

Finally, what happens when the service is over? In a best-case scenario, the congregation has a full lunch available for guests, and designated members committed to being present that week so they may interact with guests. When guests arrive, an invitation is extended by the greeter, the leader in the pulpit

Embracing Guests

during service, and a reminder in the announcements on the screens and bulletin. If the guest is still unsure, a member can invite them after the service and go with them to the luncheon, stay with them through getting food, and socialize while they eat. They are building a genuine new relationship and providing an experience of hospitality.

There are some congregations where members insist on inviting guests to their homes for lunch. While this is a gracious offer by members, consider this; most often, guests had to summon up the courage just to come to the church that day. It takes additional courage to accept an invitation to the home of someone they've never met before, for food they've never eaten before, and to stay for a period they aren't prepared for. There are better alternatives to provide guests a lunch on their first and second visit. After they have returned a couple of times, and the friendships are organic, an invitation could be extended for a personal meal at the home of a member, and thus better received.

Consider another option if your congregation doesn't have the capacity for lunch each week at the facility. What is the nearest nice restaurant to the church? Establish go-to relationships with this restaurant and do one of two things—members invite a guest to have lunch with them at the restaurant, or guests are invited as a group to meet the pastor and some other members for lunch following the service. This is the middle ground between meeting at the church and in someone's home. It's a safe third space, one that allows the continuance of hospitality to take place. An agreement can even be reached with the restaurant to provide the meals at a discount as they learn the reason for hosting these lunches and how it is part of the congregation's hospitality culture. Added benefit? Many working within the restaurant will be curious about a congregation that treats their guests so well! If this option isn't available to your congregation the day of worship, it could be scheduled for the following day, or later in the week, and an invite given to guests as part of the follow-up process.

An Honest Assessment

Most congregations think they are friendly. Maybe you as a leader think yours is. Maybe your congregation would think so, too. Thom Rainer, a respected author and church growth expert, shares some insight for those pastors and leaders who think so. "Many leaders and members think their churches have better ministries than they really do. And many leaders think their churches are friendlier than they really are."[97] I suggest self-awareness is hard for any individual, much less a congregation full of them. However, what if a congregation will place a culture of embracing guests into their DNA as part of their strategic vision. In that case, a current evaluation of overall friendliness and hospitality within the congregation needs to become a priority.

I have said it before; we measure what we treasure. Suppose your congregation treasures guests, which are opportunities to share God's love and invite them into fellowship and discipleship. In that case, it won't take much to prompt a measurement of where the current hospitality program stands. If, on the other hand, the congregation is quite happy and doesn't want new people invading their space, by all means keep things as they are.

What does a congregation measure? For one, all the external entrance points. How do the website, social media, and other external platforms look? Are they inviting, updated, and relevant? Do these various platforms let guests know they are welcome? Can people easily find needed information (address, service times, etc.)? Consider asking people who have never been to your church to evaluate the digital platforms and give their honest impressions.

Ask the hard questions about the facilities. Come in the driveway with a pair of "guest eyes" and see what they would for their first visit. Walk around the church outside and in. Make notes; take photos, be serious about the assessment of the facility and how it could be viewed by others.

If your congregation feels daring, offer a unique guest survey to be included with the thank you emails that are part of the guest follow-up program. Ten simple questions at a maximum, anonymity guaranteed. Invite respondents to be candid and open because the congregation truly wants to know, so they can become a more hospitable place to visit. Guests will likely be honest upon a request to do so, and their insight is accurate, objective, and preferred.

Another measurement is how many return guests has the congregation had? Guest retention is a significant measure of initial success with their first encounter with the congregation. If they were willing to come back again, that's good, but why did they do so? Another brief survey for return guests would be valuable in understanding what brought them back. If return guests are not prominent within the congregation, it is a strong indicator that something is not going well on their first visit.

Lastly, and one I have often employed is to ask people who do not live in

---

[97] Thom S. Rainer, *Becoming a Welcoming Church* (Nashville: Broadman & Holman, 2018), 3

Embracing Guests

the area—and have never been to the church— to come and be secret guests. Have an evaluation tool they access before their visit, including their viewpoint of the church properties and their overall visit, from initial contact through the completion of the worship services and their final exit. This is one of the most insightful and valuable tools I have used to encourage the congregation to improve in hospitality. The answers may not always be what people want to hear, but they are needed to begin addressing the issues and changing the culture of hospitality.

Guests are a Gift

One closing thought before we move on. I believe every guest is a gift from God, entrusted to the congregation when they arrive. For some who visit, this will be the first time within a church in months or years. The Holy Spirit prompted them to come to visit the congregation you lead. What will happen when they arrive? You may disagree with this, but I believe more congregations would have an increase in guests if they treated the ones they received with love and hospitality. God doesn't send broken people to broken congregations. The damage could be irreparable.

Those congregations that exhibit love, acceptance, grace, and a genuine gift of hospitality to each person who ventures into their building, are the ones God will continue to send more people to. The devil presents numerous obstacles to an individual as to why they shouldn't attend church on a given weekend. When they open the front door of your building this weekend, they have overcome all of them. What should greet them when they arrive is love, personified by greeters, leaders, and members who have accepted intentional hospitality as part of the culture.

Exhibit Christ's welcome to every person drawn in by the Holy Spirit with genuine hospitality and see what a difference it makes within the life of the congregation as it moves forward into the future.

16

GOD-CENTERED WORSHIP

Few things within a congregation bring more potential division than the content of the worship service. I am not alone in my observation. "While theological controversies swirl about the nature of justification, explanation of the Trinity, gender responsibilities, and charismatic gifts, my experience in hundreds of North American churches says these discussions are few in comparison with worship controversies."[98] While written more than twenty years prior to this book, nothing has changed as far as I have observed. Consider this: Cain's disagreement with Abel centered around worship; true worship as God desired.

Division typically centers on the style of music played during the service but extends to the liturgy, or format, of the overall service. Depending on the congregation's denomination affiliation, ethnicity, age of leadership, and other factors, the decision of which liturgy and style of music has been made. It will likely take a seismic event for it to change directions in the future. Many times, this decision has been made by a few select people who have dictated it and refuse to allow others into the conversation. Every defender of worship format and music-style points to a biblical text backing their perspective, but quite often, when one drills down to the root of the desired style, it simply comes down to personal preference. In other words, "what makes me happy." Of course, "what makes me happy" differs from person to person.

---

[98] Thomas G. Long, *Beyond the Worship Wars* (Herndon: Alban Institute, 2001), 3

God-Centered Worship

None of the decisions a pastor and leader will make within the congregation will likely gather as much attention as one involving the worship service. The fundamental of *God-Centered Worship* is vital for individual member expression and those who visit. For this fundamental to be best understood and successfully implemented within the congregation, worship as we define it may need to be reconsidered. What passes for most worship services today comes from tradition and has decidedly pagan influences. When I have shared the history of church liturgy with congregations I have pastored, they are often ready to begin an evaluation of the most critical question about worship style: is it for tradition, preference, or God's glory?

Biblical Worship

To fully understand worship, it would be wise to turn to the Bible for examples of worship. The best place to observe is how heavenly beings worship God. In the first example, John is brought into a vision of the heavenly scene of immense worship, found in Revelation 4:8-9.

"And the four living creatures, each one of them having six wings, are full of eyes around and within; and day and night they do not cease to say, "Holy, HOLY, HOLY is THE Lord GOD, THE ALMIGHTY, who WAS AND WHO IS AND WHO IS TO COME." And when the living creatures give glory and honor and thanks to Him who sits on the throne, to Him who lives forever and ever, the twenty-four elders will fall down before Him who sits on the throne, and will worship Him who lives forever and ever, and will cast their crowns before the throne, saying, "Worthy are You, our Lord and our God, to receive glory and honor and power; for You created all things, and because of Your will they existed, and were created."

These heavenly beings know God for who He is. No sin has marred their view nor placed a filter on His true beauty and perfect attributes. Satan has not deceived them and distorted the truth about God: they see Him in His eternal, majestic, awesome glory—pure and undiminished. In these verses, we catch a glimpse of true worship, giving all honor and reverence to God. It is done with a song that will be sung throughout eternity, taking no credit to the one singing, accepting no preference of how it should be sung, but giving

Leading a Congregation to Relevance

heartfelt worship to the Creator of all. It is perfect worship that reflects from the created to the Creator.

As the *Bible Illustrator Commentary* points to about this text, "The worship of heaven will be inspired by clear views of the divine character."[99] God fully seen as He desires us to see Him, instills a sense of worship to God and a full realization of who we are. True worship comes from humility, for "The worship of heaven is rendered with the greatest humility... humility is inspired by the true sense of the Divine Majesty... this humility is awakened by a due estimate of the unworthiness of self."[100] Once we fully realize who we are in light of God's perfect character, we will accept no credit for any good found within us.

While this vision to John was of worship from perfect beings, what of us who are sinners, and have never been in God's presence? What would the appropriate response be? The best example is a vision given to Isaiah, found in Isaiah 6:1-4, and his subsequent response in verse 5.

"In the year of King Uzziah's death I saw the Lord sitting on a throne, lofty and exalted, with the train of His robe filling the temple. Seraphim stood above Him, each having six wings: with two he covered his face, and with two he covered his feet, and with two he flew. And one called out to another and said, "Holy, Holy, Holy, is the LORD of hosts, The whole earth is full of His glory." And the foundations of the thresholds trembled at the voice of him who called out, while the temple was filling with smoke."

Isaiah saw this in vision, not in reality. But his response?

"Then I said, "Woe is me, for I am ruined! Because I am a man of unclean lips, And I live among a people of unclean lips; For my eyes have seen the King, the LORD of hosts." (5)

As Isaiah took in this breathtaking scene of heaven and true worship, he immediately saw himself for who he was in the light of an Eternal God. His words, "I am ruined!", are what all of us would say if we fully understood our condition and God's majesty and perfection. These words of Isaiah reflect

---

[99] Joseph Exell, Editor, *The Bible Illustrator Commentary - Revelation* (Grand Rapids: Baker, 1978), 297
[100] *Exell*, 297

God-Centered Worship

an immediate humility and self-awareness of being a person of sin, separated from God by sin, unworthy to be in His eternal presence if not for Jesus. This is what true worship inspires.

Our human response to experiencing God should be no different from Isaiah's. Still, I propose it is not our response, for we have never fully understood, nor experienced, God's character as He wishes to reveal it to us. If we did, we would be compelled to do as Moses did when instructed to "Take off your sandals, for the place where you are standing is holy ground." Exodus 3:5. Furthermore, Moses hid his face in reverence and awe of God, and God was not even revealed except through the act of a burning bush. What we lack today in our personal and corporate worship is a sense of wonder and reverence that can only come from a more profound, experiential view of God. Worship is our duty as created beings, and our response in worship reflects our relationship with God.

When leaders and members deepen their relationship with God through intentional discipleship, prayer, and further study of the Word, among other disciplines, true biblical worship can begin to find a priority within the congregation and community. It is lacking in most congregations, and Tozer was correct: "We are missing the genuine and sacred offering of ourselves and our worship to the God and Father of Lord Jesus Christ."[101] It is certainly time to bring true biblical worship back into our congregations, but most likely not the worship we are used to.

The Roots of Modern Worship

One of the sermons I enjoy preaching most with a new congregation is one regarding the church as we know it today and how it transitioned from intimate gatherings in homes to what is accepted as the norm today. One of the fascinating books written on the subject is *Pagan Christianity,* by Frank Viola and George Barna, who take most of the sacred worship cows and grind them into hamburgers. Many well-loved traditions in the church today find their roots in pagan customs introduced within the 4th Century church when Constantine made Christianity acceptable by his baptism and edicts. I've had numerous people come to me days after hearing this sermon questioning the facts (which have a historical basis) as I presented them. When they recognize

---

[101] A.W. Tozer, *Whatever Happened to Worship?* (Chicago: Moody, 1985, 2012), 10

the truth of what I shared, it begins to challenge their concept of worship—not just music, but style, format, and its true purpose.

While I encourage you to read *Pagan Christianity* for yourself, here is a quick glimpse of what we could dismiss from our current services as we know them. Pulpit, pews, entrance music and official entrance/processional of worship participants, participants on the raised platform, fine clothes from participants to observers, and a portion of the building set aside for two hours per week.[102] This small list will make the staunchest members blanche at the thought of getting rid of them from the service, and even consideration of worship within a space that is used for other programs during the week. Show members how each tradition finds its roots in pagan worship and a desire to pay homage to Constantine, among others royalty, and let it sink in. Yes, much of what is done today as tradition came from the early 300s and has survived in most congregations as liturgy and format, extending to allowed music styles. In these instances, worship has become about the worshipper, from tightly held traditions and preference, and much less about God.

I will add that once this challenging discussion begins to take place as to the root and reason for most liturgical styles and formats used today, a shift in thinking begins to take place. Where do you as a leader want to take your congregation as it pertains to worship? This can be best understood and appreciated as they mature in their relationship with God. Lastly, ask yourself: are the changes I want to make in the overall worship service, style, and content, driven by a desire to worship God or satisfy preferences I and others may have?

Define and Decide Worship

There are numerous ways to define worship, but one of my favorites is from Warren W. Wiersbe. "Worship is the believer's response of all that they are—mind, emotions, will, and body—to what God is, and says, and does... Worship is a loving response balanced by the fear of the Lord, and is a deepening response as the believer comes to know God better."[103] If we consider this definition of worship, it shifts the preferences of worship from

---

[102] Frank Viola and George Barna, *Pagan Christianity?* (Carol Stream: Tyndall Momentum), 9-43
[103] Warren W. Weirsbe, *Real Worship: Playground, Battleground, or Holy Ground* (Grand Rapids: Baker Books, 2000), 26

the participant to the Recipient. As John MacArthur insists, this is not just for the present, but "...our supreme duty for time and eternity—to honor, adore, delight in, glorify, and enjoy God above all His creation, as He is worthy to be worshiped."[104]

Worship is not defined by our preferences for style and substance but by God alone. It may take varied forms in music style, depending on culture and context, and what will be placed within the service as part of a worship spirit, but if it is not pleasing to God, it isn't worship.

What arises from this statement is a question; who decides what is pleasing to God? Who within the local congregation determines what worship will be defined as? It is a question to be prayerfully discussed by those within your congregations, praying and seeking the guidance of the Holy Spirit, Who, might I add, desires to be present within every worship atmosphere a congregation experiences. There may be an answer, though, that keeps the focus and decides many of the factors in worship.

A New Worship Focus

In *Christ-Centered Worship*, author Bryan Chappell gives some insight into the processes congregations go through to determine worship and what the ultimate factor should be. His conclusion, wherein he quotes James B. Torrance, is this: "Worship primarily driven by concerns for propriety and acceptance feeds pride and burdens hearts. This is the inevitable consequence of making anything but the grace of the gospel the soul of our worship."[105] He continues this line of thought with an additional quote attributed to Robert E. Webber, "If our worship is not an expression of redemptive truths, it inevitably drifts from being a response to God's savings acts."[106]

When we find our unity in God, we find unity with each other. Those who are currently divided according to worship style, music, and content can be brought to a unified conclusion centered on the gospel. "Even leaders who have contrary style preference can unite in a higher gospel purpose without feeling they have compromised their values. Once they see that the

---

[104] John MacArthur, *Worship: The Ultimate Priority* (Chicago: Moody, 1983, 2012), 9
[105] Bryan Chapell, *Christ-Centered Worship: Letting the Gospel Shape Our Practice* (Grand Rapids: Baker Academic), 142
[106] Chapell, 142

main concerns of worship are about meeting biblical priorities rather than personal expectations, leaders can unite behind a worship style that does not entirely match their preferences because they are convinced it advances the gospel."[107] And herein lies the best pieces of advice I have ever read or heard for congregations divided over worship style, purpose, and preferences.

The focus of worship is God. God-centered worship is what we should be pursuing for unity, relevance, and presence of the Holy Spirit within the congregation. Eternity is one long worship service!

Reclaiming Worship

I challenge your congregation to have a fresh vision for worship. Some find worship to be somewhat unnecessary. For those Tozer has a word, "I can safely say, on the authority of all that is revealed in the Word of God, that any man or woman on this earth who is bored and turned off by worship is not ready for heaven."[108] If there are indeed some within the congregation who do not like worship, I don't fault them too much: likely they have been exposed to outdated traditions and styles which do nothing to reach those within our culture today in a relevant manner.

Our worship today should define excellence, be done well, be God-focused, and be inclusive of people from every walk of life. Even the Reformers, such as Calvin and Luther, noted by Bryan Chapell, understood that worship must be accessible. "Both of these Reformers made music choices that they believed would allow people more readily to enter into the praise of God. Both eschewed the ornate preaching forms of their times in order to speak "plainly" for the people's understanding …"[109] If Calvin and Luther, among others, knew this more than 500 years ago, how much more appropriate is it for us to understand today if we are going to make worship an emphasis for all within our congregations?

This calls for a prayerful evaluation of the worship service as a whole—music, content, liturgy, format, traditional or contemporary. There may be some confines of the final decision based on local culture and denominational

---

[107] Chapell, 133
[108] A.W. Tozer, *Whatever Happened to Worship?* (Chicago: Moody, 1985, 2012), 14
[109] Bryan Chapell, *Christ-Centered Worship: Letting the Gospel Shape Our Practice* (Grand Rapids: Baker Academic), 128

God-Centered Worship

practices but pray through these, also. Let the final choices be centered on this: what will bring people to a sense of awe and reverence through worship, focusing the goal of worship away from themselves and towards God? Don't be so quick to dismiss certain music styles, whether traditional or contemporary. There may be a healthy consideration of what aspects of the service have become mere formality without any real impact on those gathered. The preacher may need to consider the sermons preached as well as the style and substance they will include. These are not bad discussions and may be needed within many congregations.

There is more to be said about worship, and many books to guide any pastor or congregational leaders seeking to understand worship better. Worship existed before creation and will continue after recreation. May we strive as leaders to reclaim worship as it ought to be within our congregations, challenging our members as David did so eloquently:

1. *"Praise the LORD! Praise God in his sanctuary; praise him in his mighty heavens!*
2. *Praise him for his mighty deeds; praise him according to his excellent greatness!*
3. *Praise him with trumpet sound; praise him with lute and harp!*
4. *Praise him with tambourine and dance; praise him with strings and pipe!*
5. *Praise him with sounding cymbals; praise him with loud clashing cymbals!*
6. *Let everything that has breath praise the LORD! Praise the LORD!"*

Psalms 150

17

Measure What Matters

As written several times previously, we measure what we treasure. Think about this for a moment. If there is a particular program, process, or project a leader prefers, they should want to know how well it is doing, and if it is realistically successful. It could be quite simple to ask those who will respond to the leader's confirmation bias, answering that "all is well, and things are swell." A leader who wants the truth will ask the critical questions of measurement and accountability to get the absolute truth.

Most congregations drift along doing the same thing week in and week out with the same results. Most I have seen are content to do so. Maybe this is an illusion. Perhaps they don't know they are drifting aimlessly because it has become a habit or tradition within their congregation. Others understand they may need a change, but they don't know why they need to change, how they should change, or the imminent dangers of remaining static. Still, congregations are frightened by what they cannot see, so they stick with what is known and understood.

Each of these responses is equivalent to the ostrich's head in the sand, ignoring what one can't see or chooses not to see. The strange thing is, no matter how much a person, leader, or member tries to ignore it, the issues within a mediocre congregation, with no progress towards relevancy, will ever go away. A congregation needs to be willing to evaluate themselves to determine their current state, and what they must do to become relevant. Doing so allows for the proper adjustments to maintain forward progress. It also requires accuracy, honesty, and diligence through the process.

Measure what Matters

Cars and trucks today are fascinating machines. At their core, they still have the same engine design principles that have existed for more than a hundred years. They have become much more complicated and computer-driven in the past thirty years. If you own a vehicle that experiences an issue and is not operating properly, you take it to the dealership or trusted mechanic. Do you want them to approach your vehicle, say everything sounds fine, and send you on your way? Maybe perform a quick diagnosis and quote a part based on what they heard in a brief listen or what you've told them? Or would you prefer they ask you to leave your vehicle for the day so they can run full diagnostic tests on it? This means they evaluate the functions of the vehicle to see what, if anything, is wrong. If something is not operating correctly, they take the needed steps to fix it.

If, as a congregation, there are no systems and processes in place to continually evaluate the functions of the congregation and its effectiveness, there will never be an impetus to change or correct what is not functioning properly. Hard to fix what no one knows is broken! I firmly believe that a leader must have evaluation tools to monitor success and avoid failure, thereby achieving progress towards the desired outcomes.

I prefer not to lead a congregation without instilling the fundamental of *Key Results and Accountability,* and I recommend you shouldn't either.

Objectives, Key Results, Accountability

These measuring components are an organic result of the *Strategic Vision* fundamental and the team that has created and sustained it. This is a required part of the strategic planning process if a congregation wants to know if they are progressing forward or in a stall. If the congregation doesn't want to know, Yogi Berra (the baseball player) is correct; "If you don't know where you're going, you might not get there." A congregation can have lots of ideas about where they are headed, and most of them do. But not everything a congregation wants to do is sustainable or practical. Thus, the need to implement objectives and key results, with the accompanying accountability. This helps to shape which ideas, programs and ministries are right for the congregation. The added benefit is accountability that allows for progress and adjustments to be measured, as well as defining a clear objective and outcome, and ultimately success.

Leading a Congregation to Relevance

Suppose a congregation decides to undergo the process of strategic vision, one that I encourage strongly and facilitate for congregations and other faith-based organizations. In that case, they have an opportunity to dream big as part of the process. If they could ask God to do anything, what would it be? Nothing is too much to ask or dream about. Then reality sets in. Of these dreams, which ones align with the as-determined vision, mission, and values of the church. Which ones can be measured? Which ones ultimately help the congregation or organization become as relevant and influential as they believe God has called them to be?

When ideas and dreams get distilled and filtered, what does the Strategic Vision Team believe are the most important in their congregation's context? They have already identified the needs of the congregation and community as well as what they would like to see God do in both. They have agreed upon a future vision that would indicate they have reached relevancy, including initiatives that will allow them to fulfill their goals. Through this process, there are chosen specific objectives and their corresponding key results, OKRs for short. Other terms would be metrics, measurements, or key performance indicators (KPIs)

Some are fearful when business practices come into church work. Still, I emphatically push back and defend some business practices and principles as wise in the business world and just as, if not more, applicable in the faith-based realm. There is a tendency by some leaders and congregations to wander along and say, "We are following God wherever He leads us, and that is good enough for us." They look back at the previous five, ten, and twenty-five years and wonder why nothing has changed, and relevancy has passed them by. They never measured to prove they were growing or took steps to correct their decline. There are major companies that use OKRs, or measurements that are similar, to determine progress and next steps, keeping them out of ruts that prevent them from moving forward. The church should be no different, from my perspective.

Putting objectives in place, with corresponding key results that measure the success of these chosen objectives, initiatives, and vision progress provides for accountability. Accountability is lacking in many congregations today, from the pastor and leaders to the individuals involved in serving within various ministries and programs. This lack of needed accountability hinders forward progress in leaders, organizations and reaching their preferred outcomes.

Measure what Matters

I have seen first-hand what occurs when there is no accountability. I have seen it in my denomination and in various colleagues with whom I served. I have observed leaders within their respective congregations falter due to lack of accountability. People often resist accountability, for it requires a deep search within, a need to provide a measurement of continuing forward progress, coupled with full transparency. Most leaders are content to drift along, achieving some things, but not all God has promised. The same goes for many congregations.

There is a need for effective coaching and mentoring for leaders today. Those leaders who pursue the right coach, who understands their context of leadership, get more done, and lead their congregations and organizations to do the same. They are not resistant to being shaped and formed as better leaders through accountability and transparency. Coaching works in sports for a reason, and the best players appreciate the coaches that developed them into champions.

As attributed to Tom Landry, former legendary Dallas Cowboys head coach, "A coach is someone who tells you what you don't want to hear, who has you see what you don't want to see, so you can be who you have always known you can be." Take a moment to assess the successful leaders you know, and you'll likely find most recognized the value of a coach to help them get there. This applies to relevant congregations too.

What could be accomplished if we took our work within the local congregation as seriously as businesses do? Businesses do it for profit and to satisfy shareholders. We do it for God, His Kingdom, and people. If the business practice of measuring for success works for them, there is no reason metrics and measurements cannot work in the church and provide needed accountability. Using them correctly helps to identify the next steps for progress or redirection.

Plan, Do, Check, Act

I want to introduce you to a most important tool if you have never used it previously, Plan, Do, Check, Act (PDCA). Where did the idea of PDCA come from? Marshall Hargrave gives a brief answer: "Originally developed by American physicist Walter A. Shewhart during the 1920s, the cycle draws its inspiration from the continuous evaluation of management practices and management's willingness to adopt and disregard unsupported ideas. The method was popularized by quality control pioneer Dr. W. Edwards Deming in the 1950s, who coined the term "Shewhart" Cycle after his mentor."[110] Another form of PDCA comes from Japan and is called *Kaizen*, "An approach to creating continuous improvement based on the idea that small, ongoing positive changes can reap significant improvements."[111] For most, the two words that best define *kaizen* are *continuous improvement*.

The company that first made *kaizen* famous was Toyota in the mid-20th Century. It soon became known as the Toyota Way. Everyone within the organization took pride in the vehicles produced and worked together to make the process better and more streamlined, to continuously work towards improvement. It was a laborious process over the middle 20th Century, but the results speak for themselves.

I won't bore you here, but reading the history of the Toyoda family, the start and growth of Toyota Automotive, and how they adopted processes that allowed for lean production and consistent growth is quite fascinating. They did not become the most prominent automotive manufacturer in the world (as of this writing) by accident. They accomplished it by measuring what matters so they could make necessary adjustments, which led to improvements and further success. In other words, they were accountable to each other, and to the overall vision, for the success of the organization.

How is PDCA implemented and best understood for the congregation? Put simply, it looks like this in practice.

> *Plan:* Selecting initiatives and objectives, with metrics.
> *Do:* Implement chosen objectives through program or process.
> *Check:* Chosen metrics to evaluate progress in a systematic way.
> *Act:* Progressing, keep going; if not, make the needed adjustments.

If Toyota, Nike, and Mayo Clinic, just to drop a few names, can use the Plan, Do, Check, Act method for growth and success, why shouldn't

---

[110] Investopia, *PDCA Cycle* (https://www.investopedia.com/terms/p/pdca-cycle.asp), accessed May 30, 2022

[111] Tech Target, *"What is Kaizen?"* (https://www.techtarget.com/searcherp/definition/kaizen-or-continuous-improvement), accessed May 30, 2022

Measure what Matters

faith-based organizations do so? Our measurement is eternal; lives that have been impacted for God and Kingdom. It should give an impetus for you as a pastor or leader within your congregation to learn how to implement Plan, Do, Check, Act as part of your congregation's growth and future success. I assure you that those who do and measure what matters are the ones experiencing the success and ultimate relevancy they have set out to achieve. OKRs, KPIs, or whichever term is preferred, are crucial to creating the needed measurements for successfully implementing the development model fundamentals, and ultimately fulfilling the strategic vision for the congregation.

Evaluating and Adjusting

As the Strategic Vision Team collaborates to formulate an overall strategy, mission, vision, and values and then brings them together with initiatives, objectives, and key results, everything seems doable. Every decision is made with the desire to align with the overall vision and mission of the congregation. The congregation's path is determined with chosen initiatives and their corresponding objectives and metrics. To determine how each objective is performing, the key results, or metrics, are evaluated in a consistent matter to determine forward progress or needed adjustments.

When establishing an entirely new strategic vision, the Strategic Vision Team must have metrics to understand how the strategic vision is moving forward. Is it being communicated clearly? Does the congregation know what the vision is? Are programs and ministries beginning to align with the strategic vision? What percentage of the congregation and regular attendees could recite the vision, mission, and values? Do people understand the purpose of the congregation? Is there an understanding of what a relevant congregation will look like in the local context?

By finding ways to measure within the congregation every quarter, you will be able to determine the success, or lack thereof, of the launch of the overall strategic vision and individual programs or fundamentals. The Plan, Do, Check, Act process can then be used to determine the adjustments, if any, needed to continue moving forward toward the desired outcome.

If during the evaluation process using metrics and key results, it becomes evident the desired progress has not been achieved, it's time to evaluate the problems that kept the key results from measuring higher. Is it not being communicated enough? Does the leader, or team of leadership, exhibit the importance of what is being communicated? What other obstacles to progress have become apparent? By looking under the hood and hooking up the diagnostic tools to fully evaluate, leadership can act accordingly to make needed adjustments for better progress during the next three-month period.

All these steps require discipline and are part of an ongoing process. They also need to be fully valued by the leader and leadership team. If, for any reason, the congregation senses or perceives what is being adopted by the congregation, be it a new strategic vision or program, is not valued by the leadership and measured as such, it won't take them long to consider it unimportant to them. Total buy-in from leadership, starting with the pastor and down the leadership line, is essential before moving any plan or program forward. It also adds weight to the accountability process which leads to the use of proper measurements for identifying progress, or the lack of it.

Why Wait?

This may all be a bit daunting. Perhaps you aren't sure this process is necessary as a leader. Maybe the process of objectives and key results cannot be easily explained or impressed upon your leadership team. But I cannot emphasize adequately the importance of placing these tools for evaluation and measurement into the congregation's processes. Without them, you and they are spinning the wheels. Measurements and accountability give an honest picture to a congregation of their accomplishments; either celebrate getting closer to the chosen destination or evaluate why the congregation was in motion but not getting closer to the goal.

If unsure where to start, there are books on the subject and professionals who can facilitate implementation. They will train you, your leaders and your congregation. God's work deserves the same amount of attention, if not more, than any business. By using tools that bring the desired results for the congregation, we honor God by doing so. Begin the process of measurements and accountability; what transpires, as a result, will surprise you.

18

Missional Influence

Many congregations today fall into the "come and see" category, also known as internally focused churches. "Internally focused churches concentrate on getting people into the church and generating activity there... what is measured is the number of people and activities within the church."[112] Internally focused congregations do so for many reasons; I believe it's most likely because doing so is predictable and comfortable. By inviting others into the congregation, there is the security and safety of the known—be it a building, program, or people. If guests are not wanted within the congregation, it is easy to push them out—if not immediately, at least over time. I have watched it happen. Internally focused churches rely on those who will venture onto the campus from an invitation of a current member, respond to external marketing, or who are sincerely seeking answers to their questions of faith.

Externally focused churches do the opposite. "Externally focused churches are internally strong, but they are oriented externally. Their external focuses are reflected in those things for which they staff and budget ... These churches look for ways to be useful to their communities, to be a part of their hopes and dreams. They build bridges to their communities instead of walls around themselves ... Externally focused churches measure not only what can be counted but also what matters most—the impact they are having outside the four walls of the church."[113]

Do you note the primary difference between the externally and internally focused churches? One plays it safe. The other takes risks. One measures

---

[112] Rick Rusaw & Eric Swanson, *The External Focused Church* (Loveland: Group, 2004), 16
[113] *Rusaw & Swanson*, 17

success by how many have come and been connected within the walls, and the other measures how many lives are impacted in the community. Of these two options, which has the more significant long-term influence?

Author Reggie McNeal, in *Missional Renaissance*, goes further in identifying traits and personalities of an internally vs externally focused church. "Internally focused churches and ministries (and people, for that matter) consume most of their energy, time, and money on a wide range of concerns, from survival to entertainment."[114] As for externally focused churches, McNeal continues, "Much of their calendar space, financial resources, and organizational energy is spent on people who are not a part of their organization."[115] One is relevant. The other is not.

The following two fundamentals, *Missional Impact* and *Community Connections*, may appear to be the same, but they are quite different. One involves intentional partnerships within current community structures and programs that benefit those whom these organizations and ministries serve. The other fundamental involves the individual members living an outward-focused life, resulting in a congregation that does the same. Both fundamentals come from the desire to shift the attention from gazing at others within the congregation (inward), to serving those in the community (outward). It is a major shift for any congregation to take, but one every congregation is called to make.

As a leader, it may be quite difficult for you, too, as McNeal recognizes. "Shifting from an internal to an external focus usually requires a radical change of mindset on the part of the leader … Many leaders have spent their entire leadership lives in pursuit of building great organizations that rise to the top of church industry standards. Changing values and motivations is not easy, but nothing less will accomplish this shift."[116] Before you can lead the congregation on this major shift, it will have to begin with you.

---

[114] Reggie McNeal, *Missional Renaissance: Changing the Scorecard for the Church* (San Francisco: Jossey-Bass, 2009), 6
[115] McNeal, 7
[116] McNeal, 7

Missional Influence

It Starts with One

As much as a leader might want to flip a switch and change the focus of their congregation from inward to outward, it isn't that simple. Every congregation consists of people, and people make all the difference. More specifically, the spiritual depth and phase of discipleship they are currently in make the difference. Individuals who deepen their walk with God begin to see people as Jesus saw them. Rather than being the priest and Levite who walked by the half-dead man on the road to Jericho, they are compelled to stop and serve as did the Samaritan. They can't help it. It becomes second nature for those transformed by God's love. As Bob Goff says, "love does," which is also the title of his best-seller and non-profit he founded.

Love cannot do otherwise. Christians are compelled by love because God's love compels each of us. Former U.S. President Jimmy Carter is attributed to have said the following: "My faith demands—this is not optional—my faith demands that I do whatever I can, wherever I am, whenever I can, for as long as I can, with whatever I have to make a difference." Isn't that the call and compulsion of every Christian? Carter's statement is founded on biblical principles, too, 1 Peter 4:10. "As each has received a gift, use it to serve one another, as good stewards of God's varied grace." The gifts all have received from God are immeasurable and undeserved. The gifts shared with others should reflect the depth of the original gifts all of us have received through Christ. Since his presidency ended in 1981, Carter has made significant impacts in the world by sharing his faith, through action, with others.

Many believers are taught to witness by word. Tell their testimony and share the story of a life changed by God's grace. Connected in some respects are then telling what they believe and why the person they speak to should also believe. Still others will be compelled to hand out tracts or books with statements of belief, done so in brief interactions or sent through the mail without any personal interaction. In each case, this is sharing through words, using story, logic, and at times argument, to persuade a person to a belief system that mirrors the individual or congregation presenting it. Personal witness that is at times impersonal but can be used with some effectiveness when done within an established relationship of family or friend.

Then some just do. Theirs is an outward-focused life. They show up where they are needed, unexpectedly: The single mom frantic with three kids and needs a babysitter ... The grieving widow ... The homeless man who hasn't eaten in days. Where there is a need, outward-focused individuals motivated by love show up. Some would say this is an empty witness, just good deeds being done, no information transferred. Consider the model Jesus exemplified. There is more record of healing and miracles than what He preached. Why may you ask? What difference can this make? "It's when we love people that God's presence works in us, and people get a better picture of God's love, mercy, and compassion. As followers of Christ. We can make the invisible God visible through our words and actions."[117] Actions speak loudly! Additionally, actions can lead to effective use of words and sharing of beliefs when asked.

When individuals within the congregation change their direction from inward-focused living to outward-focused giving, missional impact begins. It can rarely be forced but is a fruit of discipleship and an individual's walk with God. When individuals make this shift, led by the pastor and congregational leaders, a movement begins.

The Missional Congregation

There are often questions about what "missional" really means. It has been used for two decades plus at this point, yet many don't fully grasp the meaning. The best one I have found—succinct and to the point—is, "A missional church is a community of God's people who live into the imagination that they are, by their very nature, God's missionary people living as a demonstration of what God plans to do in and for all of creation in Jesus Christ."[118] I can't think of a more apt description of missional congregations filled with individuals on a mission for God. When we think of missionaries our thoughts often are those individuals who have left the comforts of their country to move to an unknown land and people. Missional congregations are also filled with individual missionaries who discover a community of unknown people who have minimal to no relationship with God and act upon it. The sacrifice may not be as great as a move around the world, leaving family and friends behind, but it is no less potent in action or results.

From experience and observations of the past 20 years, I would add that many congregations express some desire to be missional but still can't seem

---

[117] Rick Rusaw & Eric Swanson, *The Outward Focused Life* (Loveland: Group, 2009), 74
[118] Alan J. Roxburgh and Fred Romanuk, *The Missional Leader* (San Francisco: Jossey-Bass, 2006), XV

to get it done. What gets in the way are traditions, denominational structures, and inward-focused leaders that lead by preference rather than purpose. They also are congregations with long histories, set in their ways, no more able to move than the Titanic. Missional congregations and communities tend to be more fluid and movement oriented. They are more concerned with those they are called to reach than satisfying the demands of a few preference-driven people. They also resist those restrictive organizational structures, whether local or denominational, that would prohibit their missional activities. Today's most engaging missional churches are planted with intentionality or entirely reformatted with an intentional missional culture. Sometimes it's just easier to give birth than raise the dead.

What type of congregation do you lead? Would you be willing to ask the hard question of your leaders as to the purpose of the congregation's existence? What questions would you ask to identify the direction of their and the congregation's focus? Is your church a "come here" or a "go there" congregation? Is the most significant impact through programs that take place on the campus? Or is the most considerable impact felt in the community? Every congregation should be focused on the next opportunity. Who is the next person to serve? Who is the next life to impact with a practical gospel of compassion? Take time to measure the congregation's current impact and brace yourself for the most likely coming answer.

If we use McNeal's measurements regarding which direction a congregation is focused, they would be energy, time, money, and programs, with the ultimate measure being people affected. There might be some measurement that indicates work is being done within the community, but is that the focus of the congregation as a whole? It's simple, really. The checkbook is the quickest way to identify which direction a congregation is focused. What a church spends money on is what they place a priority on.

There would be some within the congregation who argue that outreach is being done within the community. Maybe they are right. Water to the homeless, running a food bank, as well as simple and effective outreach efforts that don't require too much time, are services to others already performed. If there is a desire to know how effective these programs are in terms of being missional, ask how many of those served have resulted in conversations on faith. Have there been any continued relationships of meaning? What is the goal of each activity? Know more about why the congregation is serving others and for Whom they are doing it.

Practical Missional

One of the best places to start living missional is the small groups formed within the congregation. It is easier to be more personally involved within these groups which are looking for possible ways to impact others. There are many possibilities; I won't belabor them here but research further for opportunities to provide outreach and impact. Challenge each leader of a specialty or discipleship group to commit a percentage of group meeting time to missional activity. Teach people within the groups how to live missional minded even when they aren't in an organized event within the group or congregation.

An effective way to begin thinking missional is the 2:1—>1:2 principle. Ask leaders of individual ministries to begin with a 2:1 principle of "come here" and "go there." For every two programs or events to be held for the congregation, one program or event will be held for the benefit of the community. It will be met with some resistance at first and perhaps questions about how effective the programs outside the building can be. Then the shift begins. After a specific time period ask leaders to shift to a 1:1 plan, one program/event for the congregation, and one program/event in the community. Lastly, the 1:2 punch! One program/event in the congregation results in two for the community. And just like that, a change in focus from internal to external for the congregation.

When planning events for the congregation, consider if there are places available in the community for them to be hosted. Ideally, these would be neutral sites where members and regular attendees could feel comfortable inviting family and friends to participate. Such places and locations are well-known for those within the community to find and have fewer objections coming to since they are no longer asked to enter the church. Be intentional about having leaders and members always ask how their actions can benefit the community, not just the congregation.

Missional Influence

Missional Matters

When I meet resistance from members on these new and potential changes in programs, services, and other intentional methodologies adopted to reach the unchurched better, I ask them why they object. It often comes down to what they are used to, what they prefer, what they enjoy, and are comfortable with. I share the strategic vision of the congregation to become missional, to reach the ones who are not in the church currently and may likely not come to church as we know it. Then I ask a critical question: "If the person we were pursuing through our missional culture was your son, daughter, husband, wife, or another you loved very much, who was far from God, wouldn't you want a congregation to pursue them in love, too?" When viewed through the personal lens, I rarely see any further objections to the missional refocus of the congregation. Those with complaints soon become the best supporters.

Missional is an intentional choice for a congregation. It stems from the other fundamentals being solidified within the congregation and individuals who attend. When a decision is made to be a congregation that decides to "go" as Jesus commanded, the Holy Spirit will provide divine opportunities beyond the wildest expectation of anyone in the congregation, including you!   Missional may not be something done today within your congregation but set the goal of being missional as an outcome while pursuing other fundamentals. Make it a sticky part of the strategic vision for the congregation, voted and adopted by the members. Move forward, knowing that missional will be part of the culture, and some traditions and boundaries may be broken to accomplish it. When the lives impacted are evident, missional will be a way of life for all moving into the future of relevancy.

Community Partnerships

As stated earlier, the two fundamentals in this chapter are different yet work together for a common purpose, to love others in practical and needed ways. When being missional is a choice for a congregation, there are often questions about where to start. I say start with what is already present within the community. There may be a desire to have an identity, create a new program, and make it unique to the congregation, but not always wise or necessary. As referenced in chapter seventeen, the questions would be the same for any leader starting a new program, and no different in establishing a missional ministry. It provides structure and accountability for success.

I would ask, why start something new when there are programs within the community starving for active volunteers committed to serving others? Find a person within the congregation who is gifted in organization, passionate about serving the community, and ask them to be the lead for a new type of ministry, Community Connect. It would be the responsibility of this individual and their team to begin reaching out to non-profit ministries and organizations that serve the community and explore partnerships between them and the congregation.

What are the needs? How many people do they need every week to serve others? What are the hours a person could come and assist? What is the impact within the community of the service(s) provided by the organization? What, besides human resources, could the congregation offer to the ministry or community program to aid their success?

The response will be good, I assure you. However, don't be surprised if this line of inquiry is not met with the excitement level hoped for. This won't be the first time someone reached out from a church asking some of the same questions. They likely got a short infusion of manpower and financial consideration, but what lacked was staying power. Long-term commitment should meet a long-term need. When these conversations begin, they should be followed up by in-person visits to include the Community Connect leader, pastor, and others committed to the program. Ask the organization what would be most beneficial to them. See the operations and subsequent benefits received by those individuals whom the organization serves. See if the values align with the congregation. Lay the groundwork for a meaningful partnership—not just for a week or month, but for long-term benefit to both.

Missional Matchmaker

Now the fun begins! Once the leader understands the need for manpower, such as the number of hours per commitment, time, day of the week, etc., they begin to find those within the congregation willing to put love into action. This is the second benefit of being missional through selected community partnerships. The organizations come to see the congregation you lead as salt and light, living out the principles of what is preached and taught every week.

Missional Influence

The outcomes need to be spelled out when the new program is presented to the congregation during the worship service, or even better, through small groups.

The first outcome is the people within the community who benefit. The second outcome is the missional outreach from the congregation's partnership with the ministry or program. The third is that the members of the congregation who commit to going each week become active witnesses of their faith—not what is said but what is lived! There would be no need to share doctrinal differences, persuade people by argument and scripted words, or hand each person a preferred book or tract. The witness is the life lived by the participants who are living out their missional values through the congregation's partnership in the community. These actions lead to further engagement and conversations.

As people begin to sign up for these opportunities and are active, have them share the stories of the lives they are seeing affected as a result of living missional. If the organization allows it, shoot a professional video of what is happening so it can be edited and presented to the congregation and each small group. Stories are potent persuaders in inviting others to participate in these community partnerships. It won't be long before the congregation members are as excited about participating in the program as the ministries and organizations are about having them. When these partnerships occur, they will grow in ways not anticipated.

Missional Community

When considering missional living and community partnerships, think long-term. It could be easy to feel discouraged if things don't progress far in the first year. Keep pressing and place a vision before the congregation of what will happen as they become intentionally missional and community partnerships are nurtured. These partnerships can extend to the local first responders, hospitals, assisted living facilities, public schools, and just about every conceivable opportunity leaders conjure up. This is the significant impact and influence of a choice to be missional. This is a relevant congregation—one making a difference in the lives around them, no strings attached. God will bless richly when the commitment to do so is present and continuously acted upon.

The early church was missional. In every way, they were involved in the social dynamics of the times, ands able to speak with authority when needed. Most congregations no longer have an authoritative voice when it is needed most, for there has not been a reason for anyone in the community to listen. When there are events within the community, country, or world that shake people's confidence and faith, where do they turn? There will be those who turn to their genuine faith group. What of those who have no faith group? Where will they go? Suppose a congregation is missional and involved within the community consistently? In that case, these people with no faith home will often turn to the congregation most visible—the one that was present in their lives. By the previous missional witness, they will know the congregation cares and will now turn to them for trust and a voice in uncertain times. They will turn to them for spiritual guidance.

Being missional will open avenues of unexpected influence for the congregation and its leaders such as participation in civic events previously never invited to attend, much less taken part in. It's not why the missional activities occur; it becomes a natural result of being seen as a congregation that puts community first—not just when it is comfortable, but consistently even when it is costly.

What a transition when the congregation you lead becomes the one the community turns to when they need to see God! This is missional. This is *actual* relevance.

19

THE TEACHING MINISTRY

Most Christians could easily recite the Great Commission. However, just in case you have forgotten it verbatim, here it is, Christ's final words to the disciples found in Matthew, the final chapter, "Go therefore and make disciples of all nations, baptizing them in the name of the Father and of the Son and of the Holy Spirit, teaching them to observe all that I have commanded you. And behold, I am with you always, to the end of the age." (19, 20) There is quite a bit packed into these two verses. The words we most often focus on: "go," "disciples," and "baptize." One word often overlooked is essential in the final command from Jesus, "teaching." Not *preaching*, but *teaching*. There is a significant difference between the two. Teaching is a crucial part of the last commands of Jesus and the *Teaching Ministry* fundamental needs implementation more fully in congregations.

How important is the ministry of teaching to the congregation? Consider these words by Daryl Eldridge, in *The Teaching Ministry of the Church*. "The simple truth is that the church that fails to teach will fail in its mission and will therefore cease to be the church."[119] He is not wrong. The congregation may still exist, and people still attend, but the power and influence of the congregation will have been depleted by lack of teaching. It is an urgently needed emphasis once again today for congregations. "Whatever else may be true, the church should be a gathering of Jesus' students. The church ought to

---

[119] William R. Yount, Editor, *The Teaching Ministry of the Church* (Nashville: B & H Academic, 2008), XII

be a learning community. This learning community must enable her children, youth, and adults to grow in the faith."[120] Jesus taught, so should we.

Preaching vs. Teaching

Before moving on, let's address a question some may have. Aren't preaching and teaching the same? No, they serve two different purposes, with overlap due to shared biblical content. As will be seen shortly, Jesus engaged in both at various times of His ministry. How could we differentiate the practice of teaching as it differs from preaching? "We can define preaching as the invitational and exhortation proclamation of biblical and theological truth. Teaching, by contrast, is the explanation and explication of biblical and theological truth."[121], writes author Jonathan Pennington, excerpted from his book, *Small Preaching*. He expands it a bit further, "Preaching is biblical and theological content selected and presented in a mode of proclamation with the immediate goal of invitation and exhortation ... Teaching is biblical and theological content presented in a more detailed and systematic way to explain and unpack complex issues, their interconnectedness, and their implications."[122] This may give a better understanding of each communication method and further emphasize the need for an improved teaching model within congregations.

The Perfect Teaching Model

The first model of New Testament teaching comes from Jesus. Within the Gospels, the respective writers note Jesus' teaching, Mathew being the first. "And He went throughout all Galilee, teaching in their synagogues and proclaiming the gospel of the kingdom and healing every disease and every affliction among the people." Matthew 4:23. This reference is an important

---

[120] Michael S. Lawson and Robert J. Choun, Jr, *Directing Christian Education: The Changing Role of the Christian Education Specialist* (Chicago: Moody Press, 1992), 17

[121] Lexham Press, *What is the Difference Between Preaching and Teaching?* May 5, 2021. (www.logos.com/grow/what-is-the-difference-between-preaching-and-teaching/), Accessed June 7, 2022

[122] Lexham

The Teaching Ministry

one because it adds that He was also "proclaiming the gospel," which gives a distinction between preaching and teaching. His action of teaching is mentioned over 25 times (depending slightly on the version read) within the Gospels, with Luke making more references than any other writer. Teaching, it would seem, was Christ's preferred method of sharing the principles of the Kingdom with His listeners and His process of making disciples.

Being taught was not new to the listeners; synagogues existed throughout Palestine, and those who attended the synagogues were exposed to the rabbis' teaching. Christ's teaching was different, however, as noted in Mark 1:22. "They were amazed at His teaching; for He was teaching them as one having authority, and not as the scribes." What made the difference? "The scribes taught largely by quoting other important rabbis. Their teaching was a dry rote devoid of freshness or authority. But Jesus taught out of himself."[123] The intimacy of teaching allowed Jesus to speak to each listener, giving lessons on the Kingdom and nature of His mission. Teaching was necessary to Jesus' ministry; thus, as Rick Yount explains it, "It is no surprise than that Jesus, though He preached the good news and met many physical needs, was known best as Rabonni, Master, Teacher."[124]

Early Church Model

Acts 2 indicates teaching was connected to preaching, particularly for those who heard Peter's preaching on the Day of Pentecost. After Peter preached and the listeners reacted, "They were continually devoting themselves to the apostles' teaching and to fellowship, to the breaking of bread and to prayer." 2:41,42. There is something essential to note in this text. Those being taught made a decision that resulted from the preaching of Peter. (37, 38). Teaching is not always conducted before the decision and subsequent baptism of a person but is most often a component for imparting biblical knowledge and helping the individual increase in spiritual maturity after their decision. It is ultimately a process of discipleship and continued study of theology and Christology.

What was the force of the teaching ministry as exhibited in the early

---

[123] Herschel H. Hobbs, *An Exposition of the Four Gospels: Mark* (Grand Rapids: Baker Books, 1970), 34

[124] William R. Yount, Editor, *The Teaching Ministry of the Church* (Nashville: B&H Academic, 2008), 45

church by the apostles? Is it applicable for congregations today? "The apostles' attitude was that of men who had seen a great light and found great blessing, and they yearned that other men might also see and share that which had become so precious unto themselves."[125] As noted in the text and understood as an essential principle of spiritual development in a new Christian, decision alone is not enough; imparting the education of a lifetime is a necessary component and an ongoing process of discipling.

Throughout Acts, we find references to the apostles and disciples involved in the teaching ministry, discipleship, and working with men and women to educate them in what they had come to know and experience for themselves. As each new believer grew through the process of discipleship and continued learning, they, in turn, were able to continue the teaching ministry to another generation of new converts within the church. This is authentic disciple-making.

The Teaching Congregation

It may be easy to dismiss the fundamental of *Teaching Ministry* as redundant. Indeed, teaching is taking place within the small groups, next-generation classes and weekly studies before the worship service. In all these areas, teaching is vital and contributes to the growth of those within the congregation. The placement of this specific fundamental near the top of the development model is to signify the importance of extending the ministry of teaching to those outside of the congregation through missional extension. This natural progression results from individual lives impacted by the missional living of members and community impact partnerships. They have seen the deeds, now they are interested to learn why the deeds have been done. Open and attentive, ready to learn.

Some might argue that preaching is the better format to reach these people. Maybe. Numerous congregations use preaching and evangelistic styles to share beliefs and doctrinal fundamentals with attendees. They are often told what to believe, based on proof texts and information, through the method of preaching and evangelizing. They are sometimes given a one-dimensional

---

[125] Joseph Exell, Editor. *The Bible Illustrator Commentary: Acts 1-17* (Grand Rapids: Baker, 1954), 235

view of the subject rather than exploring from different perspectives of contrast and comparison which can come through the teaching model.

Example: why Christianity? Christians know what they believe and Who they believe in. They are confident that Jesus is the Way, Truth, and Life. They read the Bible, pray, and exercise other disciplines of the Christian walk to be a more mature disciple. When sharing this belief with others, they present it as concrete—as if saying, "I have found the solution, this is it, and you need do no exploring on your part to accept what I am telling you." We live within a new attitude today because this is fast becoming the "show-me generation," not the "tell-me generation," and their preferred model is teach, not preach,

There is wisdom in understanding and applying apologetics here. Why would we come to a better understanding of Islam, Buddhism, Taoism, Hinduism, and other major world religions? Competency in the other world religions doesn't mean a Christian has accepted them; it means they compared the other ones and contrasted them with Christianity to see which brought them to the truth they were seeking. Teaching allows imparting this learned knowledge to the listener to engage in thoughtful questions so they can arrive at a personal conclusion.

Preaching is a one-dimension conversation and doesn't provide much room for reflected dialogue with listeners. As we progress deeper into the 21st Century, I sense from listening to the younger generations a resistance to being told, "this is what you should believe" rather than an invitation to converse through dialogue, teaching, and learning. Frankly, I have come to realize I much prefer being taught rather than told. I am not alone in this, I suspect.

Teaching allows the audience to share curriculum and content in many areas. Reaching people within the community using varied teaching programs allows further congregational relevance in their lives. Today we face greater mental health challenges than previously known. A mental health expert available to teach personal mental health and wellness classes would be appropriate. Health challenges present another problem for millions today; popping prescription pills isn't the answer. Courses for health and wholeness, with practical actionable teaching for the listener, provide real solutions that better their lives.

There are so many other areas of curriculum and content to benefit those in the community who are willing to let the congregation speak based on what they have seen in practical witness. The quickest way to find out what the community needs most is to work with a company or consultant that does community demographics. You will quickly have a window into the community's needs and can address them with professionals who are trusted and have the skills to teach others. When those who attend classes learn the teacher and curriculum can be trusted in practical everyday matters, they will permit discussion on spiritual matters as a result.

Teaching as Culture

Adopting the *Teaching Ministry* fundamental is crucial for the congregation, and it starts with the pastor as a teacher. Most pastors feel called to preach, proclaim, exhort, but are not sure they have the gift of teaching. If you think this isn't your gift, seek to grow that gift and talent or give permission to those in the congregation who do have the gift to lead in developing this ministry. When choosing a curriculum to specialize in, find people with a recognized authority in the area who also have the gift to teach. A person may have the gift of teaching, but that doesn't mean the gift is helpful in teaching everything if they don't have proven knowledge and success in the subject. Those who teach best have firsthand knowledge of the subject they are teaching and can be a respected educator in the listener's mind.

Teaching within the congregational setting ultimately is to bring people to a better knowledge of the Bible, God, and maturity as disciples. It is a fundamental worth investing time and resources in as your congregation seeks to become an even broader influence within its community, engaging in pertinent conversations.

20

DECISIONS & DISCIPLESHIP

Being a relevant congregate revolves around people. Jesus died for people, and for people He established the *ekklēsia*. In the congregation's work, it is imperative to focus on what matters most; the individual decisions made for God and the process of discipleship which allows each to develop spiritually. The fundamental of *Decisions and Discipleship* may seem redundant, yet it is essential as the congregation moves up the development model. Earlier in the model, the fundamental of *Intentional Discipleship* was discussed, primarily as it pertained to the congregation's existing members, the work of small groups, and how the process would continue assimilating new people.

This fundamental is similar, yet still different. As the congregation moves towards a missional culture, there will be numerous opportunities to interact with individuals on a life journey of faith. Some will be atheist and agnostic; others once were firm in their faith and have let it fade, and still others would say they are believers. Each person on the continuum is making decisions about their faith, or lack of it. They may be reinforced in their mind by what they believe, or by interacting with your congregation's missional outreach, they are likely beginning or continuing to make decisions that bring them closer to God, or conversely, away from Him. The fundamental of *Decisions and Discipleship* applies to them, and the congregation as they work with these individuals without regard to where they are on the continuum.

Decisions, Decisions

Often it is tempting to think there is only one definitive decision made by an individual as it relates to God. Will a person accept Jesus and the gift of salvation He provides, or will they not? Much has been written about getting people to this decision. Often it is witnessing what God has done in the life of the person sharing, asking the person being witnessed to if they would like to experience the same, and leading them in the sinner's prayer. If they agree to do so, everyone celebrates and counts it as another lost sheep who has been brought home.

While these moments are beautiful, is this the only decision that led an individual to cross over from a life without God to a life with God? I say no, it is not. Life is made of numerous small decisions every day. For part of this chapter, we'll focus on those decisions predicated on relationships with the congregation. These could be through the interactions of your members living with an outward-focused mindset and their relationships with family, friends, co-workers, and random people they meet.

The other alternative is the congregation's work with community partnerships and how people interact within these environments. Perhaps it is the missional outreach programs that are making a practical impact as individuals focus on those whose needs, they can meet. For others, it could be the provided classes with subjects that are meaningful to them, part of the teaching ministry of the congregations. Whichever connecting point made it happen, from being a guest at worship, small group participant, or recipient of missional work within the community, each causes a person to make small decisions about God, whether positive or negative.

Could we be honest? As Christians, we have not always given the best representation of Christ to the world. I've seen "saints" on the weekend become "sinners" on the weekday. I have seen it looking in the mirror first but hearing stories from others who experienced the same, some broadcasting it far and wide on social media. When we as Christians are less than what we have been called to be as disciples and committed Christ-followers, and our actions and words look no different than the world, people make decisions about Christianity, and, ultimately, God.

The brief negative interaction could give them pause about becoming a Christian and distort their view of God. Every moment of a Christian's life

Decisions & Discipleship

is a witness for or against God, whether realized it or not. Every moment causes someone else to make a small decision about God, whether for or against, based on the interaction they just experienced. A person who is not an active Christian may determine there is no benefit to believing in God, as they witness a Christian act and behave no differently than they would under the given circumstances.

When hurting people walk into a church on a given weekend, what will they encounter? Will there be warmth and acceptance or judgmental looks and rejection? Each response leads the person who entered to make a small decision at that point about God. Will they walk towards God as a result, or be pushed away? How many stories have been told of individuals who experienced both types of response when they came to church? Those welcomed with love and acceptance felt grace and compassion, drawing them closer to God. Their small decision from this encounter led them to God, while the other individuals were pushed away from God by those who were unwelcoming when they arrived at church. They decided against God from that encounter, and that small decision led to further decisions against God and life without Him.

One must be fully aware of how every interaction with another individual leads them to small decisions. The goal of the missional congregation, with missional members, is always to lead people toward God or further in their walk with God, depending on where they stand on the one decision that matters above all others. What we say and do can be the most decisive influence on small decisions that lead a person in a positive direction as it relates to God. What are we doing today as congregations to influence these small decisions?

The Joy of One Decision

Many experiences bring me joy as a pastor, but none like those involving people who have decided for God. There may be different ways to phrase it, "accepting Jesus," or "inviting Jesus to be in your heart," or others more familiar, but I say it is a statement of belief regardless. The person responded to the Holy Spirit's work within their life and presented with the promises of God for all who believe; they decide to do just that—believe. This decision seems as if it should be more involved than just belief, and it is, but belief is the

Leading a Congregation to Relevance

measure Jesus used for those who make the decision for Him. "As Moses lifted up the serpent in the wilderness, even so must the Son of Man be lifted up; so that whoever *believes* will in Him have eternal life." John 3:14-15 (*emphasis mine.*) It is a decision of belief in God, the gift of salvation offered through Jesus, and the life which comes as a result. Many decisions will continually stem from this most significant one, but none carry the weight of the decision to believe and receive the gift of eternal life (John 3:16.)

These decisions for Jesus should be anticipated and celebrated! It's what we exist for as spiritual leaders and congregations. Yet, in numerous congregations, the decision has been less-than-anticipated and, at times, considered inconvenient. I could not find the baptismal tank in the congregation I arrived to pastor at several years ago. I was eventually told it was a portable unit and had been taken down and put into storage. Within sixty days we had it set up, ready to fill with water at a moment's notice. It stayed set up the entire time I was there. In the next two years, there were twenty baptisms, while only five had occurred in the previous three years. The difference? The congregation anticipated the decisions, and when those happened, they celebrated. I stood up each week and shared a vision of what mattered most; decisions made for God.

Another congregation had their permanently installed tank used as a storage compartment; it had been years since they performed a baptism. They were not actively anticipating decisions for Jesus and the resulting baptism. Was it no wonder the congregation was dying? Sadly, their mindset never changed much, although we did get the baptismal tank cleaned and ready for its intended use.

The other side of the proverbial coin is those congregations that actively anticipate decisions and have celebrations when they occur. I also have experienced this; energy pervades the congregation and attendees when they go home, and it leads to even more decisions. In these congregations I have pastored, we were excited about the small decisions, which led to the one decision that mattered. When a person decided to enter a new life in Christ by putting their complete confidence and belief in Him, we were ready the following weekend if necessary, and we celebrated! There weren't numerous questions asked about their understanding of all the biblical beliefs, or ones our denomination considered fundamental. These would be included with the

Decisions & Discipleship

teaching ministry to follow. I had one criterion for baptism, a solidly biblical one, found in Acts 16.

"And he (the jailer) called for lights and rushed in, and trembling with fear he fell down before Paul and Silas, and after he brought them out, he said, "Sirs, what must I do to be saved?" They said, "Believe in the Lord Jesus, and you will be saved, you and your household." (29-31, emphasis mine). There it is. One decision to be made, a culmination of all the small decisions made to that point, and the start of many small decisions to be made as a person grows in their relationship with God. All centered on one word: believe. Everything that comes from this one decision, anticipated and celebrated, is now the beginning of intentional discipleship. This is where the person begins to learn the deeper spiritual truths and grow in their walk with God every day.

Decisions and Discipleship

The next verse from the ones previously quoted says, "And they spoke the word of the Lord to him together with all who were in his house." Acts 16:32. Paul and Silas immediately began the process of discipleship which is effective teaching that leads to a person's continued spiritual growth. This is the same process we as congregations should be undertaking. A person decides and immediately we enter them into intentional discipleship. It may look different within varying congregations, but each congregation should have a culture of intentional discipleship. The method may be one-on-one with a spiritual mentor of the same gender or a designated small group for those taking the first steps in their Christian walk. Whichever method is used, be intentional, and be immediately ready to engage in this process.

I will refer you back to chapter six for a more detailed explanation of why I believe intentional discipleship should be fundamental in every congregation. Still, I will add a few things here regarding discipleship as it applies to those responding to missional outreach and the evangelistic efforts of the congregation. Firstly, what should the process of biblical discipleship achieve? Some suggest it is an imparting of knowledge to a person. Does this person know the biblical beliefs that are essential? Perhaps these are the ones the congregation or denomination they joined understand to be the most important. In this process of discipleship, what is the measure? Knowledge.

Yet how many Christians exhibit a whole lot of biblical knowledge without revealing a whole lot of Christ?

Perhaps the most succinct measure of discipleship is this, "The distinguishing mark for discipleship is a transformed heart, transformed affections."[126] For many, this goes against the grain of what they believe the discipleship process should be. It would require a change in process and emphasis within their local congregation to achieve. But let these words admonish and inspire you; "Don't settle for information or behavioral modification. Aim for Christ-centered discipleship that brings about true transformation."[127] This is what Jesus taught and what every discipleship process should involve: transformation.

When individuals have made their decisions for Christ and embark on their new journey with Christ, there will be many who want to have a say in their process of growth. I call these people the self-appointed conduct committee These individuals demand an immediate change in dress and appearance. Some will ask about the new believer's habits, expecting smoking and other possible addictions to be dropped immediately, then judging the person's decision as not real if they can't produce the immediate changes demanded. They expect every person who accepts Christ as Savior to make quick and long-lasting changes in their life. Hardly. It is a process. A sponge can quickly soak up dirty water, but it takes constant rinsing and wringing of the sponge to get it all back out. Such is life for all of us. We will be transformed on the journey of discipleship, but for most, it will take longer than twenty-four hours after the decision.

A Different Discipleship Approach

Imagine if Jesus, within gathering his twelve disciples, told them about his coming death, resurrection, launch of the church, the disciples' persecution, their changes in behaviors, and for most of them, a martyr's death. Most likely, each would have split immediately. Rather, Jesus spent three years taking them on a journey. Read the accounts through the Gospels and see Jesus revealing truths through His example and teachings. He told them what they needed to know as they matured and were ready for it. Eventually, it all took root, and

---

[126] Eric Geiger, Michael Kelley, and Phillip Nation, *Transformational Discipleship: How People Really Grow* (Nashville: B&H, 2012), 30

[127] Geiger, Kelley, and Nation, 31

they were anointed on the Day of Pentecost which launched the early church into motion. Had Jesus revealed everything within the first days of His time with them, none would have been around to experience what God would do through them.

One thing troubles me more than any other within congregations I have pastored, individuals I have met, and colleagues with whom I have worked—a tendency to forget that many of us have been on a spiritual journey for some time. Today we experience God in different ways than when we first believed. There is spiritual maturity. As we grow, our experiences are more profound and the tests of faith more intense. The growth didn't come overnight; it was through time and process. Yet, we place this expectation on new Christians, expecting them to act the same, and pushing them off into life with God, all without the discipleship needed for maturity. We wouldn't let a child drive a car on the highway just because they can see over the wheel. They don't have the maturity to make decisions that come from age and wisdom and being taught how to drive and make those decisions.

The same applies to those who are new in their walk with God. They are, after all, "spiritual babes." They drink the milk of biblical truth because they aren't ready to cut their teeth on steak. Keep this in mind when forming processes of intentional discipleship for those new believers who have just made the most important life decision. The most significant aspect of their spiritual growth is a new knowledge of God and how in their life, God is ever-present and will walk them through whatever the devil brings. Rest assured, when a person decides to choose Christ, the devil and his army of fallen angels are ready to do whatever is necessary to make them regret ever making the decision. The discouragement may come from family, friends, co-workers, or other established relationships. It may be through other circumstances—a loss of job, friendships, or other painful predicaments. What they don't need are well-intended people within the church doing the devil's work for him.

I urge your congregation to have a process of intentional discipleship for new believers if it is not in place currently. Provide friendships, mentoring, and groups of people who understand a believer's journey and will treat them carefully and in the spirit of Jesus—with grace, tenderness, love, compassion, and friendship. This is a most critical, sensitive work and one many congregations have failed in. They either are too intense, with high expectations placed on the new Christian, be it a change of habits or an increase in knowledge and understanding of fundamental beliefs, or they go the opposite direction and have no provided discipleship program.

I am not sure which is worse. But if I had to choose one, I would say having no implemented discipleship program. We would not leave a human baby to fend for itself; we should expect nothing different from spiritual babes. They need mature, transformed disciples within your congregation who understand the process and have walked in their shoes. Those who have experienced God's overwhelming grace will mentor through grace to another. Welcoming new believers into their family is a special privilege for a congregation. It's the entire congregation's responsibility to ensure each new believer has a safe environment to grow and experience grace as the Holy Spirit leads in each of their lives. It begins with you as the leader to set this into the DNA.

A Warning

Having new disciples within the congregation can be quite daunting. As I have stated, it's a special privilege given to every congregation, but not all are ready for it. Welcoming new disciples requires a significant dose of grace, love, and acceptance. Being there for individuals who are learning how to walk spiritually and will fall often is a privilege. When they fall, there should be others close by to help them get up, not kick them while down. For some unknown reason, many Christians are compelled to do just that.

As a leader, you have worked on the development model to cultivate a new culture for the congregation. It takes time. Most congregations are not ready for the process of new disciples immediately; that is why this is at the top of the model. It comes after a congregation chooses to be intentionally outward-focused and missional. It also comes after processes have been established to strengthen relationships, transmit biblical truth, and nurture believers in all stages of their walk with God. If all the other fundamentals have been implemented and are successfully working, then being missional, and interacting with others far from God, will be a natural outflow. The personal decisions and new journeys of discipleship will be expected and celebrated.

While nine months is the gestation for a baby to grow within a mother, it is also a suitable time for the parents to prepare for their incoming child in the home. They fix up a new room as a nursery, fill it with the appropriate furniture and decorations, and provide an overall safe environment for the

Decisions & Discipleship

baby. Other decisions are made, too, all with the new child in mind. So it is within your congregation. Every decision and action made previous to this fundamental has been to welcome new spiritual children into the family of God. A congregation can't do the latter without preparing through the former. They should also do the former in preparation for the latter. Expect and anticipate decisions for God and begin a walk of discipleship with those who make them. Everything done up to this point is to prepare your congregation to be the welcoming environment to which God will bring people. I have witnessed firsthand what happens when the Holy Spirit leads individuals seeking God to a specific congregation because He can trust the members to treat them with grace and patience on their new journey.

Is your congregation ready for those God will bring to you? If not, don't rush it; set the culture and become prepared through the steps of the fundamentals I have laid out. If the fundamentals have been successfully implemented, culture instilled and ready to welcome new believers, then God will bless as the congregation moves forward. The greatest reward for any congregation is being entrusted with raising up new disciples.

21

Exponential

When every fundamental has been put into place, the congregation is ready for the ultimate experience, exponential growth, and multiplication. Seriously, if a congregation isn't growing and creating new congregations, it isn't healthy. Or it's just being selfish. There is often a desire to grow large for the measurement of numbers, but with significant numbers come new issues to deal with. The trend of larger churches seems to have reversed as of late, with smaller congregations being planted and sustained appropriately. This is the best for spreading the influence within new communities. Also, purposefully planted congregations allow the processes discussed in the previous chapters to begin again. The ability to equip even more people for service and intentional leadership is exponentially better!

The *Exponential Impact* fundamental is the fruition of all the other fundamentals successfully laid down from the foundation to the pinnacle of the development model. The vision is seen to its maximum impact— missional multiplication if you will. Ready to duplicate the process in another congregation or extend the culture and DNA of the current congregation. Put simply, healthy congregations multiply and reproduce. To add emphasis, I would strongly state every congregation should be intentional about being exponential, and work towards that goal with every decision made.

Elmer Town and Douglas Porter agree: "The church is a living body. Just as everything that is alive will grow and reproduce, so your church should be growing and reproducing itself by starting a new church. Just as God originally created all things to reproduce... so your church can double its ministry

Exponential

by planting another church."[128] Healthy congregations must reproduce to continue in relevance and expand their influence within new communities. This is a continuation of the "Go" within the Great Commission.

The Temptation of Numbers

Wouldn't it be nice to pastor a church of many people listening to your sermons each week? Who hasn't watched a pastor on streaming and dreamed of filling up a stadium of those who clamor for all you have to say? This is the selfish view of growing a large congregation. In many ways, it isn't healthy. Consider some of the large congregations within the United States. I won't mention a specific one, but how many of those thousands in attendance are engaged and equipped for ministry? Many hear a sermon from a renowned speaker, then disappear into the shadows until the following week. Many missed opportunities come from large congregations.

In some cases, the denomination wants the congregation to exist in order to keep the influence within one location. As Ed Stetzer and Daniel Im write, "For many the idea of one large church is more attractive than multiple churches. Large churches have the resources and programs to be full-service congregations. Thus, many leaders think the most efficient denominational strategy is to help medium churches become large churches."[129] While this may be considered a wise strategy in some cases, you will see in a moment that there is a way to keep the influence and structure of a large church and still be exponential.

Many pastors have done their best work in small congregations. For some reason, however, as leaders, we have been taught unconsciously to believe we have "arrived" and are doing our best for God when the numbers are significant on the weekend. It's time to dismiss this line of thinking and consider the power of influence, engagement, and movement. I've pastored congregations of different sizes, and the most effective ones were around 100-150 in attendance. I also have been in a congregation of more than 1,000

---

[128] Elmer Towns and Douglas Porter, *Churches that Multiply* (Kansas City: Beacon Hill Press, 2003), 7
[129] Ed Stetzer and Daniel Im, *Planting Missional Churches* (Nashville: Broadman & Holman, 2016), 7

people, a preacher-driven church for many. However, many were still engaged in active ministry and made purposeful attempts to engage even more.

The size of the congregation does not matter to God. The issues of relevance matter most. Small congregations can be just as relevant, or even more so, than larger congregations. I am repeating this to reinforce it. Don't dismiss the small congregation you may currently be pastoring. Understand also I am not disparaging large congregations. They have their place. If all of pastors want the large congregations, who will be left to share their spiritual leadership with the smaller ones? These members of smaller congregations need quality, God-led spiritual leadership, too.

The new measurements are relevance and influence, seen through the people whose lives are changed due to the ministry of the congregation you lead. That congregation may be twenty-five people now, but you are given the privilege to engage them in ministry as a leader. You can take the principles of this book and push forward with a vision of what's possible in the small congregation, with a missional culture embedded. Small congregations can be just as relevant as large ones and exponential as well.

Purposeful Multiplication

The early church centered around Jerusalem and Judea when it started. Severe persecution dispersed the early followers of The Way further out of their comfort zone which then planted the seeds of the gospel in even more distant lands. Guy Waters further expands upon this concept: "This dispersion likely involved these believers' longstanding removal from Jerusalem to neighboring regions. As Luke goes on to show, these believers were active in bearing witness to Jesus in their new homes."[130]

Accumulating members in one congregation is not essential to God. That can lead to complacency and comfort which is never good for starting or sustaining a movement. Had the disciples and early Christians kept themselves within their known community without dispersing, they would be like most congregations today that are inward focused rather than outward focused. Most congregations are content to remain as they are, growing in one place

---

[130] Guy Prentiss Waters, *Acts Study Commentary* (Leyland, England: EP Books, 2015), 202

Exponential

because it feeds the desire to be preference driven, comfortable, and happy rather than purpose driven.

I suggest the congregation's strategic vision laid out by the Strategic Vision Team and voted by the members should be intentional to expand beyond the current location within a specific time frame. This vision defines an intentional decision to grow and multiply with a relevant mission in the existing community, a new congregation planted in another community, or through multi-site campuses. All three are God-led, but I favor multi-site because it keeps the original congregation's working DNA intact and shared with the new campus. It's a method that allows the congregation to grow with solid leadership and the development of a new group of individuals on the new campus site. It also has the advantage of keeping the strength of programs and processes intact, yet with broader influence. Whichever way the congregation feels led to expanding, becoming exponential must be a clear objective. A non-negotiable part of the vision is a clear destination of being exponential, and frankly, the last measurement to determine the congregation is fully relevant.

Putting metrics (or OKRs) into place can help determine how well the congregation is moving toward the intentional goal of being exponential. When this intentionality becomes communicated as part of the church's overall vision, some individuals will offer immediately to be sent out to begin the new plant or multisite campus. If they offer their leadership and spiritual gifts for the new church plant or multi-site campus, accept their willingness happily and start the process of training them as apprentices to key leadership within the current congregation. When the day comes to send the next group out on a quest for exponential growth, they will be ready to go, replicating the processes and DNA instilled by congregational leaders and yourself.

Mission to the Forgotten

I would offer another suggestion for exponential growth. There are many churches in rural areas of the United States which are dying. They need an infusion of leadership and committed lay members. Those with energy who are equipped, and ready to work within the community each congregation resides. You may know of some congregations within your denomination or discover others as you pray about this and are led by God to find them.

Rather than accumulate engaged members in one congregation, consider challenging members to become missionaries. This can be done with smaller congregations that are just getting by with five to ten people each week. What a difference having twenty-five to fifty new people engaged could make in the direction and future of the congregation! Not all congregations need to be birthed, as many are waiting to be fostered or ultimately adopted so they can grow to be healthy and relevant.

I would also add that this cannot be forced on these small congregations. They have pride and many are tied to the traditions of their congregation. If this approach is to be successful, it must be done with prayer and a very soft touch. A small congregation already knows they cannot do what needs to be done within their community. They are just surviving at this point. A new vision of what's possible needs to be introduced, with a missionary group meeting with the small congregation to dream of the potential future together and to learn about the church's history and the remaining members.

Learn and understand about the community with them. Use a demographic study to gain insight into the needs and preferences of individuals who reside within a specified territory or zip code of the congregation. Share with them the current DNA of your congregation, the mission and vision God has placed on the hearts of individuals within the congregation, and how it could align with the small congregation. Get them excited about what God wants to do through their small congregation and then ask if they would like to be adopted as a multi-site campus of the larger congregation. Becoming a campus will benefit individuals and families who would like to make this small congregation their home, working alongside the current members in engaging their community, and breathing new life into a dying congregation.

This is just an idea to consider, but I believe many current congregations would gladly consider it. They face becoming irrelevant, if they aren't already, in their communities otherwise and would be open to the possibilities. If this idea is appealing to you, research it further, for there are more things to consider in making this a successful venture for all.

The Mission to Extend Influence

As I wrap this up, I do so with a continued challenge to reach the goal of being exponential. Please don't allow your congregation to become selfish and bloated in its current location when it's called to multiply and influence new areas where the mission needs to be extended. We are a rapidly growing world. It may seem like there are more churches than needed, but what is needed most are churches that are intentional about discipleship, engaging people in mission, and drawing people to a deeper desire for God. Suppose the congregation you serve is healthy and has successfully implemented the development model to reach the pinnacle of exponential growth. In that case, you owe it to the congregation to challenge and lead them to multiply by church plant, multi-site, or adopting a smaller congregation.

22

THE MODEL CONGREGATION

I understand if all of what has been read is somewhat overwhelming. I would encourage you to consider that much of what is included within this book may already be taking place within your congregation. What's different within the development model is the priority and placement of each fundamental and how they relate to, and strengthen, another. Yet know also that each fundamental is important individually. The model just brings them together in a more organized and effective manner.

You may seem overwhelmed if you consider it your responsibility to undertake everything. I would refer you to the fundamental of *Leaders and Teams* and how investing in both areas will provide the leaders and volunteers needed to witness each fundamental succeed. Leaders must help members discover their spiritual gifts, identify their talents, and harness their passions, all to be used for the mission. Then a leader invests in the next generation of leaders, who continue the process. The goal is for a congregation of fully engaged members working in the areas that fit them best for the outcome of being relevant to their community.

A Matter of Perspective

There are multiple views on the development model to be taken. The 50,000' perspective gives a broad overview; the 2,000' deeper dive explains why each is important in the life of a relevant congregation. The challenge

The Model Congregation

of each leader and congregation is to drill down even deeper into each fundamental and contextualize it by community and culture, among other factors. Find best practices that allow the fundamentals to succeed within the congregation—methods, and ideas relevant to the demographics of the congregation and community. The twenty fundamentals give much room for further exploration on a street-level view and implementation locally.

Quite often, you as a leader will need to zoom out and take another 50,000' view of how the fundamentals lock together and why some fundamentals need to be strengthened before others can be focused on. Encourage leaders within the congregation to go through this model, and regardless of the fundamental area they are focused on, invite them to take an overall view of how their fundamental area is relevant to the others within the model. It is quite natural to get so focused on one area that the reason for its existence becomes lost.

Finding the Way

If you find the development model useful, let it be a compass for personal leadership as you move forward. Consider it ever-present in congregation leadership sessions, elder meetings, or appropriate consultations where direction and implementation of the congregation's mission and vision are discussed. To arrive at the ultimate destination a congregation chooses, it always needs to be reminded of where they are in relation to that destination. The model can also be pointed to as the purpose for decisions and priorities within the congregation. You decide.

Implementation

This model, and each fundamental, is for you whether fresh within the congregation as a pastor or as another congregational leader. Maybe it's a decision to revitalize the church, which while difficult is not impossible. Whichever it is, I believe this development model can be helpful, as can each of the fundamentals by themselves. It's a model and may be adjusted as preferred. It also needs to be owned by not just you as a leader but your leadership team and, eventually the congregation. You may question how soon they should know the intent of this model and how to implement it. I say as soon as you are able. Invite leaders to read this book to understand how everything fits together and each fundamental's purpose, placement, and importance. They will very soon see that this model is important when *Christ-Centered Preaching* and *Member Connections* are a priority to you.

When sharing the model with the congregation, I suggest the best time may be when you begin to introduce God's vision for the congregation. Perhaps not the placement of the fundamentals within the model, but the overall importance of each one in the congregation living out its mission and achieving its vision.

However you decide to adopt this model, in whole or in part, let it be done with the leading of the Holy Spirit and much intentional prayer! With that confidence, you will not fail.

23

BEFORE YOU GO

The challenge of being a spiritual leader within the congregation is serious. Be you a pastor, elder, deacon, or a leader with a minor title and more spiritual influence; God has entrusted much to you within the congregation and community. "Leadership is waiting for you every day... It's waiting for you to act. It's waiting for you to show others that you mean what you say. It's waiting of you to demonstrate that you know how to get people moving."[131]

Everyone within your congregation and community is an opportunity for you to demonstrate the truth of God's character and encourage them to gain a more profound knowledge of God. Every individual you meet is another opportunity for intentional discipleship and an invitation to join you on the journey. Patiently model, mentor, and teach them so they, in turn, can do the same with the next generation of disciples and leaders behind them. I cannot think of a more significant work to be involved in—being a spiritual leader is a call to be taken seriously, a life to be lived fully committed.

We are in a time of upheaval in earth's history. As I was writing this week (May 2022), the tragic story in Uvalde, Texas, unfolded. An eighteen-year-old stormed into the elementary school and ultimately took the lives of nineteen innocent children under the age of eleve4n. Tragically, two teachers died trying to save and protect the lives of the children in their care. One cannot turn on the news without hearing disturbing reports. Jesus' words are more potent than

---

[131] James M. Kouzes and Barry Z. Posner, *The Truth About Leadership* (San Francisco: Jossey-Bass), 105

ever as it relates to end times, "And because lawlessness will be increased, the love of many will grow cold." (Matthew 24:12).

This is an urgent time for congregations to be influencing their community for Christ and being relevant. Genuine Christians can live out the principles of the Kingdom of God, being salt and light in a dark world, demonstrating by action that love is the better way, even in the icy glare of hate and wickedness. Church buildings open with individuals inside who welcome others with a spirit of grace, mercy, unconditional love, and acceptance. There, attendees will find inviting conversations on faith, a way home for the unbelievers, and hope. Today's relevant congregations can be a "map" for those seeking meaning, purpose, and answers.

Called to Go

Jesus commanded His disciples to go, which has been applied to all disciples throughout the centuries. Through the synoptic Gospels, the command is the same; "go." Tell the world, share the gospel, and bring Jesus to the people and people to Jesus. Don't rest until the last sermon is preached, the final truth taught, the last person baptized, and the last disciple has been made before He comes. Jesus made a promise for His church, the *ekklēsia*, at Caesarea-Phillipi; he confirmed the purpose and foundation of the church in Acts, "But you will receive power when the Holy Spirit has come upon you, and you will be my witnesses in Jerusalem and in all Judea and Samaria, and to the end of the earth." (1:8).

Ultimately, every believer within every congregation, no matter denomination, is to be a living witness of the gospel of grace and Christ's redeeming love. The changed lives of people are the greatest testimony of the effect of the Cross and Christ's atoning sacrifice. This is the saving, redeeming work of Jesus for all humanity, and on a more personal level, you and me. No one is exempted. The gift is extended to anyone who accepts. It's our responsibility as the leaders within congregations to let our members know they have been called out from the world. They have been sent on a mission to make the gift of redemption known by word and deed to everyone, no exceptions.

Jesus has all power and authority over every congregation on this planet today; He is the head of all collectively and individually, your congregation

Before You Go

included. The same Holy Spirit that lit the church on fire in the first century is ready to light yours on fire, too. The secret is simple. Just as the early disciples united under Jesus, engaged in earnest prayer, and waited for the Holy Spirit to come at the appointed time, your congregation is called to do the same. But they can't do it without you. Every work of God has a spiritual leader driving it forward to a vision of completion.

Your Spiritual Leadership Matters

Your congregation needs you. They don't just need your presence, your sermons, or your chairmanship at the next board meeting. They need you engaged in a personal, authentic, transparent relationship with God. If you did nothing else for the next 30 days after reading this book, take a sabbatical to refresh and connect with God in a very meaningful way.

That would be the best place to start moving your congregation forward. The most significant movers and shakers in the church's history over the past several centuries have been men and women connected to God, reflecting an authentic relationship with Him. They would not move without Him. They would not minister to their congregations without bathing everything in serious and persistent prayer. Are we not as spiritual leaders in need of the same today? Yet we try to get by with so little of God while we accomplish much for Him, leaving us to wonder why our successes are so limited. When will we ever learn? We are trying to accomplish Christ's remaining work while excluding Christ from the work.

I will admit that in pastoring for twenty years, I often failed at being fully immersed in a serious walk with God at times. My relationship with God was growing and developing as I matured. I still had the view of a God who demanded my best and perfect acts prior to His blessings of love, grace, and forgiveness. Then through several experiences, I began to understand God to be so much more than I knew Him to be. This revelation of God's true character—as I began to understand it—started a new phase of ministry for me. While I grew deeper and lived with transparency and authenticity, I saw the change within my congregations.

Surprisingly to me, though, God blessed my ministry to others despite me, when I was weak in my spirituality. I'm so glad God doesn't allow our poor fitness in ministry and leadership to be a reason our efforts can't reach others. Despite us, God continues His work through us to others. What could be accomplished if our relationship with God was deep and personal? What if we spent the disciplines of prayer, Bible study, meditation, worship, service, and more to engage with Him and cultivate a deep and abiding friendship each day?

The True Secret of Success

The secret of success is abiding, as Jesus told the disciples. "Abide in me, and I in you. As the branch cannot bear fruit by itself, unless it abides in the vine, neither can you, unless you abide in me. I am the vine; you are the branches. Whoever abides in me and I in him, he it is that bears much fruit, for apart from me you can do nothing." John 15:4,5.

Imagine a relationship of abiding in Christ, one so close that you, with humble boldness, could ask as Moses did, "Show me your glory." (Exodus 33:18). This is the result of constant growth with God.

Beyond asking God for a glimpse of His glory, Moses asked for something even deeper before requesting to see Him. Moses asked, "...if I have found favor in your sight, please show me now your ways, that I may know you in order to find favor in your sight." (13). This should be our urgent daily request as leaders while we live out the call God has placed on us. When we realize we know nothing and God alone is our Wisdom, Knowledge, and Strength, then we will have become the spiritual leaders He needs. We turn away from our dependency and lean in on His. Our congregations will note the difference, and the Holy Spirit will descend as a result, rekindling the fire so the work may not only continue, but conclude.

Parting Word

This book is principally fundamentals, with "how-to" mixed in for clarity and examples. Techniques used to flesh out the fundamentals are to be done in the local context. Methods come and go; fundamentals never will. It is tempting to be swayed by the next big thing in ministry methodology, catch the wave of something others are doing, and ignore what God is calling you to do within your congregation. Whenever I have been tempted to jump on the

Before You Go

next big thing or follow the next great leader, I am reminded by E.M. Bounds of what God wants most from us as leaders:

> *"We put it as our most sober judgment that the great need of the Church in this and all ages is men (and women[132]) of such commanding faith, of such unsullied holiness, of such marked spiritual vigor and consuming zeal, that their prayers, faith, lives, and ministry will be of such a radical and aggressive form as to work spiritual revolutions which will form eras in individual and Church life. We do not mean men who get up sensational stirs by novel devices, nor those who attract by a pleasing entertainment; but men who can stir things, and work revolutions by the preaching of God's Word, and by the power of the Holy Ghost, revolutions which change the whole current of things.*
>
> *God can work wonders if he can get a suitable man. Men can work wonders if they can get God to lead them. The full endowment of the Spirit that's turned the world upside down would be eminently useful in these latter days. Men who can stir things mightily for God, whose spiritual revolutions change the whole aspect of things, are the universal need of the Church."[133]*

Are you that man or woman God has called? Today you are needed more than yesterday. Will you yoke with Christ, surrendering self and trusting fully where God leads? He will fill you beyond capacity with what you need for these days—what the church needs in the broadest sense, and what your congregation desires in the narrowest sense. Quit worrying about what the individuals within your congregation, your denominational leaders, and the world thinks of your leadership; lean on God for instruction and affirmation. We must depend on Him if we are to accomplish what we have been called to do. I pray for you, as for myself, that we will be the men and women "Whose spiritual revolutions change the whole aspect of things." May it be your prayer as well.

---

[132] Please note the use of "man", or "men" in the general sense, not in omission of women.
[133] E.M. Bounds, *E.M. Bounds on Prayer* (Kensington: Whitaker House), 520,521

A Quick Note …

I would appreciate connecting with you! Feel free to email (connect@therelevantcongregation.com) to discuss further what you have learned in this book, challenges in ministry, or how I can help you in the context of your ministry. I am also available through our company, Faith Development Partners, to work with your congregation or faith-based organization. We provide coaching, team building, strategic vision, fundraising guidance, and organizational development services. To learn more about what we offer, visit us at www.faithdevelopmentpartners.com

If you would like further resources for your congregation, you may locate them at www.therelevantcongregation.com They are free for those who have purchased the book and provided on the honor system. From how to find the next pastor for a congregation, build a ministry team, and engage members, to other applicable resources, they can be accessed on the website.

I have also included on the website resource page a list of books that apply to many of the subjects contained here within these pages, as well podcasts and other media that could be helpful for every leader.

I sincerely hope this book was a blessing. May God bless your leadership and the congregation(s) / organization you serve, with the goal of spending eternity with those we have been called to serve and share God's love with.

With gratitude,
Dean Waterman, MBA